If Your Water Cooler Could Talk ...

Organizational Engagement:
Getting Beyond Employee Engagement

Dr. Jim Bohn

Jim Bohn holds a doctorate in Leadership from the University of Wisconsin-Milwaukee and is the author of research on organizational transformation published in multiple journals. A regular lecturer at the University of Wisconsin-Milwaukee, Concordia University, and Marquette University, his previous books include *Architects of Change: Practical Tools for Executives to Build, Lead and Sustain Organizational Initiatives, The Nuts and Bolts of Leadership. Fixing A Broken Team, Improving Management Effectiveness Through ProAction, and the Art and Science of Middle Management.*

If Your Water Cooler Could Talk …
Organizational Engagement: Getting Beyond Employee Engagement

ProAxios Publications
855 Ulao Road
Grafton, WI 53024

Cover design by Brian Holz - Atomic Design

Editing and interior design by Emerald Design Co.

Publication Date: October, 2019

ISBN-13: 978-1-70178-987-6

ISBN-10: 1701789876

Dedication

To my high school English teacher, Raymond Vils, who believed in me.

Endorsements

"Having an engaged workforce has never been more critical to achieving our strategic goals. We introduced the Organization Engagement assessment tool to our business in 2018 as the first step in our newly created Human Capital initiative. The survey results allowed us to align our global leadership team and validated several key transformational opportunities to improve our organizational performance and our overall business results. Any company looking to take their Human Capital Management to the next level would benefit from utilizing this approach to an engaged workforce."

—Rob Hoglund, CFO and VP of Finance, Vernay

"I liked the metaphors of water cooler! Besides the smoking shed, the water cooler area is one of the few places in the organization where 'purity' still exists. The six elements of Organizational Engagement transcend cultures and can be universally applied. It moves away from the traditional survey of getting ground-up feedback and trying to fit into the bigger picture. Organizational Engagement starts with the 'Big Why' as a beacon for all employees to align their vision with the organization's vision. Well done!"

—Raymund Chua, Managing Director, Heraeus, Singapore

"'People are our greatest asset'" is a common notion spoken by good leaders every day. Good leaders also understand the employee engagement metrics for their organization, but that isn't enough. Great leaders are the ones who really believe people are their greatest asset and want their organization to thrive, so they ask what is our Organizational Engagement? Dr. Jim Bohn does a masterful job distilling a wealth of research to make the case for Organizational Engagement. Jim also leverages many real-life experiences that will resonate strongly with people from all industries and organizations offering sound advice and guidance that will immediately help your organization improve.

—Mike Markiewicz, Director, Executive Programs UW-Milwaukee Sheldon B. Lubar School of Business

"It is time to refresh decades-old employee engagement concepts. Dr. Jim Bohn's approach delivers a fresh, new view of employee engagement which looks outward into the organization and targets more precise and actionable engagement factors. Organizational Engagement thoughtfully explains why traditional employee engagement measurement does not address real challenges in pinpointing employee engagement issues and offers a solution for employers who are ready to take a new approach."

— James Kerpan, Senior Vice President, Human Resources

"If Your Watercooler Could Talk is a fantastic road map for executives to follow. It clears away the dense fog surrounding this subject. The reader can follow the critical aspects of organizational engagement with each item being well documented, sourced and mapped out for execution. For those willing to take the leap, the employees, you, and the investors will be glad you did.

— Jim Smith, Organizational Consultant

"Dr. Bohn has harnessed the material that every OD practitioner and leader needs to know with this book. A must read for enhancing organizational performance."

— John T. Eggers, Ph.D., President, Transitional Goal Achievers, LLC

"Dr. Bohn hits one out of the park again, writing a very easy reading book on how to change your organization's culture. Excellent guide with a lot of good information and links."

— Michael Sekula, VP, Global Supply Chain Mgt. & Safety Inpro

"Dr. Bohn vastly expands what's already known about employee engagement and provides what's missing: an integrated organizational level perspective. Dr. Bohn challenges old assumptions about employee engagement and broadens our understanding of how people, organizations and all the myriad of structural variables work together. Bohn connects the dots between operations and business outcomes. His approach offers timely, applicable and essential insight to help businesses change, thrive in our new and oftentimes challenging marketplace and most importantly, grow."

— Sandra Nichols, Associate Professor, Concordia University

"Employees who have faith in their company and their leaders will apply discretionary effort to make certain they are a part of a winning team: yours. This book outlines the value of gathering data about the bigger picture perceptions of your people and then provides actions you can take to get employees wanting to drive the value of your business whether you measure that by ROI, reduced absenteeism, increased productivity, revenue or others."

— Jay Held, Vice-President, Learning and Professional Services

Acknowledgements

A book like this is a project of shared knowledge. I like to think I laid the foundation, but without insight from other intelligent people with skill and experience in the marketplace, this book would be missing significant details and analysis. I count it an immense blessing in my life to know so many wonderfully intelligent and thoughtful leaders.

Greg Wilgenbusch has been a fantastic partner in this journey, providing insight, helpful critique, and guidance, in addition to encouragement along the way.

Mike Markiewicz, Director of Executive Programs at UWM, offered some important corrections early in the project and helped me make a major course correction in the writing.

Supriya Desai of Desai Transformation provided me exceptional feedback early in the project. The coaching she gave me was extremely helpful. I am *so grateful for her guidance.*

Dr. Don Kirkey put forth incredible effort on the technical content of this book. He graciously helped with detailed analysis and bibliographical research. Don knows these waters and has been exceptionally helpful in the formation of this book.

Lisa Howard, a friend and finance expert, provided the chart concept relating the six elements of OE with specific financial goals. She also provided important input on an initial draft.

Tony Cortese, former SVP of People Services at Herman-Miller, offered exceptionally sharp insight. Grateful for his critique and thoughts regarding Organizational Engagement and HR.

Lisa Raebel, Founder and Chief Storyteller at Rebel Girl Marketing, LLC, offered specific and helpful guidance on how to sell this mind-shift to leadership in the HR chapter.

Dr. Hilary Curry read and commented, providing specific guidance on framing the concept of OE, and also offering her global vantage point.

Monte Pedersen, Principal at The CDA Group—Leadership consultants, offered guidance during the very first stages of the book and encouraged me to continue. I'm grateful for his help along the way.

Patrick Cline, PhD, provided insights after an exceptionally detailed reading of the manuscript.

Jim Smith, Organizational Consultant, provided critique specific to executive responses and also comparisons to employee engagement.

In addition, I would like to thank the following people for reading and responding to the book at various stages of development and commenting on the drafts: Sandy Nichols, Vincenza Capone, researcher; Tonille Miller, Global VP of Culture and Engagement; Mike Sekula, VP-INPRO; Paul Schulz, President and CEO at Max Weiss; Tom Lowery, Legrande Holdings; Courtney Dvorak, Continuous Improvement Consultant; Bob Van Der Linn, HR expert; Laura Tate, SHRM-CP I-O practitioner, Heather Younger; J.D., Lynne Coles Vice President, Growth and Chief Marketing Officer SCMA – Canada; John Eggers, PhD; James Kerpan, SVP HR; Jay Held – VP Learning and Professional Services, Rae Forrest Smith, and Ken Farer.

Primary Consulting Access to the BOES

Organizations seeking to use the **B**ohn **O**rganizational **E**ngagement **S**cale© are directed to Human Capital Mentors who provide primary access to the instrument and process.

greg@humancapitalmentors.com

(847) 867-7451

www.humancapitalmentors.com

Foreword

Behind every successful business is a vibrant dynamic organization that engages and energizes employees. As a seasoned Human Capital executive, I have worked with large and small and public and private companies to create and execute strategies to address the engagement of our teams. I've learned that neither you nor your employees can force workplace engagement. It must be ingrained in your business and embedded within each individual employee.

In *If Your Water Cooler Could Talk,* Dr. Jim Bohn draws on his extensive academic and business background to identify a new and practical approach to this elusive goal. He starts by reminding all of us that businesses are not formed for the sole benefit of an individual but for the broader good of all stakeholders—customers, employees, and society.

All leaders have blind spots about themselves, their teams, and their overall business that prevent them from reaching their full potential. These blind spots will manifest themselves in chronic organization issues that cannot be adequately addressed by traditional employee engagement approaches and will result in employee disengagement. Once this fundamental flaw is identified, we can take a new, more strategic approach—Organization Engagement. There is power in trusting and leveraging the collective insights of your employees about their view of the strengths and opportunities of the organization and your organization's ability to achieve outcomes: the "we" as identified by Dr. Bohn.

With this foundation, he goes on to identify and outline six key organizational elements in a logical, straightforward manner, creating a roadmap for business leaders and Human Resources. He takes the time and effort to fully explore each element, providing clear definitions and explaining its impact on the organization and providing the non-organization development practitioner the ability to understand and implement meaningful actions.

There is no silver bullet when it comes to engagement. There is only good management, strong leadership, a solid dose of reality, and hard work. This effort is supported by the concepts, practical approaches, and insights gained from making the strategic choice to engage your workforce by focusing on Organizational Engagement.

— *Greg Wilgenbusch*
President, Human Capital Mentors

Preface

L eaders are perpetually in search of the Holy Grail of organizational performance, yet the same chronic organizational problems persist. Unless those problems are directly addressed, organizational outcomes remain the same. It is critical for leaders to ignore the latest popular management fad and focus on the non-novel—the *plain*, *direct*, *straightforward* elements of organizational behavior that make a real difference in performance. The endless stream of articles on LinkedIn are evidence that chronic organizational issues exist and have yet to be solved.

Though organizations may differ in their products and services, their chronic challenges are very much the same across time and location, because human nature is the same across time and space. In my four decades in the corporate world, I continually observed the same problems repeat themselves over and over again, irrespective of markets, geographies, and product lines.

If Your Water Cooler Could Talk is distilled from my decades of hands-on leadership of teams, academic research and graduate level teaching, personal observations in many of the Fortune 500, and my writing and speaking. This book provides you with an alternative to employee engagement and a playbook for transformation focused on the chronic issues that all organizations face.

The book is a combination of research and practice. Each section includes brief empirical studies that serve to ground the advice I offer. Each chapter provides hands-on analysis and specific operational actions to improve your organizational performance.

Executives have not seen the results expected by Employee Engagement, and thus it is time for a fresh approach to organizational analysis. **Organizational Level Engagement** addresses the behaviors that make an organization tick—it is a step beyond employee engagement.

The skeptical executive might ask: "Well, isn't this just another flavor of the month?" Not at all. Here's why: Organizational Engagement focuses on the deep, chronic, year in-year out, decade-in/decade-out problems that have plagued companies forever. OE directly addresses the six essential behaviors at the core of organizational performance. These are not "soft skills"—*because there is no Holy Grail*, there is only hard work focused on six key elements of performance.

OE gets to the heart of what people are talking about at your water coolers right now and provides a path for dramatic organizational transformation. Find out what people are saying and use their insights to radically transform your company today.

— *Dr. Jim Bohn*
October 2019

A Note to Senior Leadership

"Initiatives fail because they are hosted too far from the top."

—*Jim Smith, Organizational Consultant*

When an executive team decides to proceed with an Organizational Engagement study, they hold the key to success. Providing a clear action plan built from executive support is the key to increasing organizational momentum and change. Senior executives set the pace by modeling the changes they seek in the organization—it is seldom about what you say and often about what you do.

You ask: *"Why is this any different than any of the other programs I have heard about for years?"*

Answer: Because it directly addresses the chronic issues all organizations must master to improve performance. There is no magic here, no silver bullet—just hard work around six key areas of company performance.

You ask: *"What am I going to get out of this?"*

Answer: Your organization will focus exclusively on specific elements of organizational behavior with the greatest impact on performance and employee motivation.

You ask: *"How will this improve cycle times for product and service development?"*

Answer: The six elements of OE are the bedrock, foundational behaviors that make your organization tick no matter what new developments are taking place.

You ask: *"How will OE reduce turnover and ensure we are an employer of choice?"*

Answer: If you attend to the six elements of OE, your organization will improve its performance. Everyone wants to be with a winner.

OE is your playbook.

If you see a need to move quickly in your organization, the Snapshot Analysis in Appendix A (page 200) will give you a head start.

If you start this, follow through.

Table of Contents

Dedication iii
Endorsements iv
Acknowledgements vi
Primary Consulting Access to the BOES viii
Foreword ix
Preface x
A Note to Senior Leadership xiii
About the Author, Dr. Jim Bohn xvii
A cautionary tale: Transfer industries xviii

SECTION I— ARGUMENT

Chapter 1:
Organizational Achievements Require Organizational Level Evaluation 1
Chapter 2:
It's Time to Move Beyond Employee Engagement 19
Chapter 3:
Chronic Organizational Problems and Business Distresses 34
Chapter 4:
It's time to rethink engagement 47
Chapter 5:
Organizational Engagement:
What you'd hear if your water cooler could talk 50

SECTION II— ANALYSIS

Chapter 6:
The Six Elements of Organizational Engagement:
Your Transformation Playbook 62
Chapter 7:
Element #1: Clarity of Mission 65
Chapter 8:
Element #2: Workforce Cohesion 71
Chapter 9:
Element #3: Communication 87
Chapter 10:
Element #4: Conviction to persist: Resilience 102

Chapter 11:
Element #5: Leadership Commitment   110
Chapter 12:
Element #6: Consequences   120

SECTION III— ACTION

Chapter 13:
The things leaders must do to manage Organizational Engagement   133
Chapter 14:
HR's role in Organizational Engagement and a Case Study   143
Chapter 15:
The Six Elements of Organizational Engagement   154

SECTION IV— APPENDICES

Appendix A:
Six Elements of Organizational Engagement   161
Appendix B:
Methods of Organizational Analysis   164
Appendix C:
Workshop harvesting   169
Appendix D:
Bandura's Theory of Efficacy   175
Appendix E:
A review of the distresses
along with detailed analyses for improvement   176

References   179

About the Author, Dr. Jim Bohn

Dr. Jim Bohn has organizational expertise and insight stemming from decades of successfully leading leaders. His business insight derives from observing the organizational behavior of multiple Fortune 500 organizations, ranging from hospitals and healthcare, to retail and finance, to manufacturing and telecoms.

He served in a variety of roles in the corporate world beginning in 1973, personally leading the transformation of multiple underperforming teams to achieve award-winning levels of success. Retiring after 33 years with Johnson Controls, Dr. Bohn launched his own Change Management and Organizational Transformation Practice. Dr. Bohn has a unique blend of hands-on, in-the-trenches experience in addition to a rich pedigree of research from his Ph.D. studies.

In addition to lecturing at local universities, he is the author of several books including *Architects of Change: Practical Tools for Executives to Build, Lead and Sustain Organizational Initiatives, The Nuts and Bolts of Leadership, Getting I.T. Right: Installing the Organizational App,* and this work, *If Your Water Cooler Could Talk.*

In addition to his published research, his teaching at the Lubar School of Business at the University of Wisconsin, Milwaukee, Concordia, and Marquette, along with his work in organizational transformation, he has led hundreds of workshops, spoken at the Milwaukee Business Journal, The Paranet Group, the National Academy of Change Management Professionals, and led workshops for SHRP and Wisconsin I/O Psychologists, ASTD-Twin Cities, Atlanta Field Service Conference, Metro Milwaukee SHRM Annual Conference, IFMA Twin Cities, and the Chicago Corenet Real Estate Group among others, including PMI International, Minnesota PMI, National Association of Credit Managers, the Plant Facilities Management Association, Johnson Controls, Kohler, GPS Education Partners, The Medical College of Wisconsin, Wisconsin Energy Corporation, VERLO Corporation, American Packaging and many others.

A cautionary tale:
Transfer industries

"We need a better way."

CEO Jennifer Stampleton walked into a room of a hundred directors and middle managers at Transfer Industries, a multinational manufacturing conglomerate. "Well, everyone," she announced, "it's that time of year again. We will be conducting our Annual Employee Engagement survey. I know I can count on everyone for their cooperation."

The half-hearted smiles and low enthusiasm around the room belied a veiled frustration with the annual process. Even the doughnuts and coffee weren't making much of an impact.

Dale Argent, SVP of HR, studied their body language and felt adrenaline shoot through his body. He calmed himself and chimed in with a bit of forced professional enthusiasm. "We'll have all the forms online again this year," he added, "so employees will find it very easy to quickly fill out the survey and get us our results. Once we have those, each of you will be responsible to work with your teams to develop action plans and submit them to us by the end of the month. We look forward to working with everyone. Watch for several emails of instructions in the coming week."

People could sense his slight hesitation when he asked, "Are there any questions?"

A hush fell over the room until it was broken by Bill Smith, Engineering Director, and twenty-year veteran of Transfer Industries, who raised his hand. "Do we intend to do anything differently this year? I mean, our employees are so familiar with this process, and we nearly always get the same data and expectations. Nothing changes for them except some small items, and they know they're checking a box. People are literally inoculated against this stuff."

Bill was highly respected by the other leaders. He had outstanding performance, his teams loved him, and his track record was impeccable. But there was little he could change about the annual Employee Engagement Survey except do what was asked. He wished there was another way to improve organizational performance.

The participants ushered out slowly, bracing themselves to talk to their team members.

Jennifer Stampleton turned to Dale Argent: "Can you stick around for just a minute?" Dale walked over and they both waited until the room cleared. "You know, Dale," Jennifer said pensively, "Bill has a point. We've been doing this for a long time, and we both know the numbers haven't appreciably changed. We can't get the needle to move on the data."

"Maybe we need a new consultant or a new survey tool," Dale responded, looking for a way out of the conversation (and seeing more work ahead).

"No, no, that's not it," Jennifer replied. "We need to stop measuring at the individual employee level and start focusing on the organization."

Dale said, "I don't think anything exists that measures organizational level engagement."

He was wrong.

SECTION I— ARGUMENT

Chapter I

Organizational Achievements
—— Require Organizational Level Evaluation ——

▶ **Leaders continually seek tools to create organizational transformation.**

▶ **Chronic problems impact all organizations.**

▶ **Organizations exist to provide broad societal benefits, including employment, products, and services.**

▶ **Organizational financial viability exceeds individual employee needs.**

▶ **To improve, organizations require organizational-level evaluation.**

Leaders continually seek tools to create organizational transformation

Leaders know their organizations cannot stand still. Organizations must continually improve. They must change for the better—or vanish. Selecting effective tools to create transformation is an ongoing pursuit for all executives, because today's organizations are facing powerful global competition, a dramatically changing labor force, new technology including AI, and generationally different expectations.

Research shows that successful, powerful organizations pay more, provide more and better benefits, and offer greater job security and employee satisfaction, thus reducing turnover and absenteeism. In other words, *organizational performance heavily influences employee satisfaction.*[1] "Candidates want to work for companies that provide a solid footing and are poised for growth. The more stable they view an organization, the more likely they may be to see a future with it."[2] In the end, *it is the organizational level that matters most.*

---

1   Schneider, B., Hanges, P., Smith, D., & Salvaggio, A. (2003). Which comes first, employee attitudes or organizational and financial performance? *Journal of Applied Psychology, 88* (5), 836-851.p. 847.

2   Gallup, *State of the American Workplace*, 2017, p. 28

The stuff we have yet to fix

Savvy leaders know that chronic organizational problems exist within their companies and in other companies they have served. For example, leadership and communication are perennial challenges within *all* organizations, but those elements never quite get the attention they deserve from consultants or employee engagement surveys. Endless articles about leadership and communication on LinkedIn are evidence that chronic organizational issues exist and cry out for resolution. So those chronic, ongoing challenges continue to test the enterprise.

Executives *know* that formalized change programs have value and tend to "lead to change that cannot be matched by merely flexing regular operating procedures."[3] However, leaders also want to ensure that their transformation methods produce a positive return on investment. Leaders stake dramatic human effort, finances, and time to create deep transformation, because they know transformation requires strenuous effort that goes well beyond business as usual.[4]

And that's just for starters. Executives expect even more.

---

3   Reeves, Faeste, Whitakee, Hassan. *The truth about corporate transformation.* MIT SLOAN management review 2018

4   Reeves, Faeste, Whitakee, Hassan.

Executives want organizational transformation methods that achieve the following:

1. They **address specific behavioral issues** that impact organizational performance.

2. They are **strategically powerful across an organization**, providing enterprise-level metrics that are precise and clear and that also demonstrate dramatic change.

3. They are **realistic in assessing the complexity** of an enterprise.

4. They are **generationally agnostic**—not relying on refining policies that only address specific generational needs.

5. They are **based in research** yet are understandable within the organization. (There are no clichés or odd quirky phrases.)

6. They provide HR with a straightforward method for strategic organizational improvement, and therefore **elevate HR to be a true strategic partner.**

7. **They introduce strategic change that considers the *we* not the *me*.** In other words, they are no longer focused on the individual employee, but on all employees working together to strategically improve the organization.

8. **They are true organizational diagnostic tools** and not just another check-in-the-box program.

In short, leaders want the investment of transformation effort to produce better organizational results and strategically position their organization for even stronger growth in the future.

Let's begin at the beginning: Why do organizations exist?

Here's a fundamental question: Ask any organizational executive what they consider to be the ultimate goal in their work. Most likely, they'll tell you, "The *ultimate* goal of my work is *the success of the organization*. It's about the survival of the business in the face of competition. It's about profitability. It's about sustaining the business and maintaining employment for team members. It's about creating shareholder value. It's about *winning*. I want my organization to thrive and accomplish the strategies we develop." *Harvard Business Review* writers agree: "What matters is winning. Great organizations—whether companies, not-for-profits, political organizations, agencies, what have you—choose to win, rather than simply play."[5]

Though the organizational level matters most, we continue to assess companies at the employee level.

Organizations serve stakeholders and customers, along with employees, *but organizations do not exist for individual employees.*[6] This is not a cynical, unfeeling statement that disregards employee concerns. At its root, it is a profound statement of the desire (and need!) to sustain a business over time, to help it succeed under mounting local and global pressure, to orient new technologies and societal challenges toward the goal of providing continued employment for organizational team members. The fact is: *Organizations need to survive at the organizational level, not at the employee level.* Yet, strangely, organizations continue to focus on the individual employee as the data point for organizational improvement.[7]

Employee engagement researcher Zinta Byrne states an obvious yet critical truth: "For organizations to compete, they must produce, and this holds true around the globe."[8] Business has always been about the effectiveness of the **enterprise**, the **organization**—not the needs of any specific department or individual. Companies that have been around for over a hundred years demonstrate that sustaining the organization is a key leadership goal that transcends individual employees. *Yet we continue to diagnose organizations at the level of the individual employee.*

---

5   Laffley and Martin, *Playing to Win*, p. 5; HBR, 2013
6   If they did, there would never be terminations, new hires, transfers or promotions – an organization would simply keep the same employees. As one of my former bosses said, *"We are not an employment agency."*
7   In my opinion I believe part of this emphasis comes from a constant discussion about individual needs and wants in our marketing, advertising and communications over the past 20 years.
8   Byrne, p. 128

The employee is at the center.

Consider the graphic in Figure 1. The employee is at the center of employee engagement, with an exclusive focus on employee needs and concerns in their local environment. And with an Employee Engagement survey, employees are given *more* reasons to focus on themselves and their own personal setting and leadership. *Frankly, the questions employees are asked lead them to conclude that they are the center of what is happening in an organization.* And, while every person in an organization is important, *their own personal concerns do not drive organizational performance.*

Figure 1. Employee Engagement

The predominant focus of most organizational improvement methods today is the *individual level*, using employee engagement as the primary tool of analysis. Studies show that while over 70% of companies conduct employee engagement surveys, less than 30% are satisfied with the results. Yet, though employee engagement remains the primary approach to organizational analysis, it is an elusive concept to define. The most up-to-date research laments this fact: "Employee engagement is a challenging concept to describe and study because it seems to manifest itself in many ways, defying initial attempts to box it into a single and simple definition".[9] If the definition is unclear, it is unlikely to improve organizational performance.

9   Byrne, p. 3

Business-level achievements require organizations to fire on all cylinders.

Enterprises thrive when all the moving parts are working together to achieve business related financial outcomes, including:

1. ROI (return on investment)

2. Managing Opportunity Costs (productivity and turnover)

3. Process costs (waste, inefficiency, cycle time)

4. Growth (margin and revenue)

5. Innovation (initiating new and revolutionary concepts and products)

6. Leverage and Scale (making 2+2=5, increasing employee productivity)

No single employee can bring about the financial and business achievements listed above. It takes an entire organization to accomplish complex strategic financial and business goals. Lots of things are happening to bring about those organizational achievements. Consider Figure 2. Each of these activities in this graphic are a component of organizational activity (and there are *many* more).

Figure 2. The many components of organizational activity

Figure 3. The organizational level is the key to success

Figure 3 shows the dramatic complexity of an organization.[10] Each of those boxes represents dramatic leadership, communication, collaboration, and accountability efforts. An organization's ability to work *together* to achieve goals and produce output is the heart of organizational success. This includes, but is not limited to recruiting, hiring, training, planning, recognition and reward, and strategy and tactics, with a heavy reliance on managing and coaching. It includes, above all, measuring the effectiveness (or ineffectiveness) of departments working *together* to (1) develop products and services, (2) market effectively, and ultimately (3) accomplish an organizational strategy. *The amount of <u>effective</u> effort being put forth by the organization to accomplish organizational strategies is the determining factor in organizational success.* How an organization interacts *as one* to achieve outcomes is the key to success. That has been true over time for corporations developing every imaginable type of product and service in every geography across the world.

So, what makes an organization tick?

As a leader, you've pondered this question many times: What is happening at the *organizational level* to bring about the financial accomplishments, completed projects, and strategic achievements the organization desires (and needs) to survive in a highly competitive environment? Is the organization operating in the most efficient manner to achieve organizational goals?

It is not the efforts of individual employees that bring about organizational achievements, but *the coordinated effort of individual employees* working in concert to achieve something bigger: in psychological parlance, we call that a **superordinate goal**.

So, what makes an organization tick? What is necessary at the organizational level to bring about the accomplishments, completed projects, and strategic achievements desired by the organization? As a leader, you *know* employee engagement reflects the amount of effort being expended by the *individual*, yet that does not resolve your concern about what makes your organization tick.

---

10   Even small businesses are managing similar actions on a reduced scale.

Employees know when an organization is not operating effectively.

Members of an organization can sense their organization's capability to achieve outcomes. It's what they talk about at your water cooler. They *know* when something is not right. "It's not the job that causes me stress, it's the emotional toll I experience navigating organizational nonsense to get the job done." They *know* when effort, funding, and precious human motivation is wasted. They know when leaders are ineffective. They know when strategy is failing. They know that they are not informed about critical information. They know whether people are held accountable for bad performance or outcomes. And they pay close attention to how their leaders manage these issues at the organizational level.

But leaders may not pay attention to their employees' deep concerns.

As a leader, does it ever cross your mind that your employees are talking about these things? Maybe you're not hearing it directly, but people are talking about their concerns in the halls of your organization, at the cafeteria table, next to the coffee machine, at local pubs --- and in your parking lots. Wouldn't you like to have a way to use that input to re-create and transform your enterprise?

So... what if your water cooler could talk?

The humble water cooler is a hub for conversation. It is a place where employees gather to discuss what's *really* happening in their organizations.

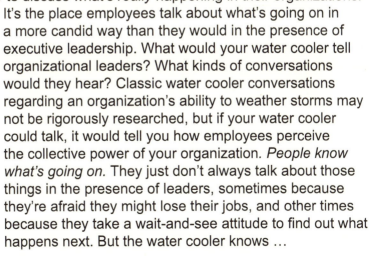

It's the place employees talk about what's going on in a more candid way than they would in the presence of executive leadership. What would your water cooler tell organizational leaders? What kinds of conversations would they hear? Classic water cooler conversations regarding an organization's ability to weather storms may not be rigorously researched, but if your water cooler could talk, it would tell you how employees perceive the collective power of your organization. *People know what's going on.* They just don't always talk about those things in the presence of leaders, sometimes because they're afraid they might lose their jobs, and other times because they take a wait-and-see attitude to find out what happens next. But the water cooler knows …

The water cooler would tell you it heard things like this:

"I'm not so sure we're going to make those fourth-quarter projections; we don't have the product offering ready."

"Not enough sales in the pipeline, I hear."

"I wish this place would take more time with promotions—they seem to elevate some real fruitcakes."

"Did they really change the insurance plan again? I can't believe it—I wish they'd told me ahead of time. My family is in trouble now." "

This company is in big trouble—there is no way this company will exist in five years." All those statements are cognitive appraisals of an organization's effectiveness. *Those appraisals deeply impact employee motivation.* People will work hard for winners but will wait and see if they sense their organization is losing ground.[11]

You and I know that those conversations are going on right now. Your employees have an intuitive sense of your company's mission, how your company is doing in the marketplace, how it weathers storms, and the effectiveness of its leadership. *The answers to those questions influence the amount of effort employees are willing to expend.*

If your employees have an overall sense that your company knows where it's going and is well led, *they are likely to exert more effort to accomplish organizational goals.* But it is simply impossible to know their appraisal of your organization (and its ability to activate motivation) using tools focused exclusively on the individual employee.

Even more interesting to this author is that Employee Engagement survey data often contradicts what's really happening, what's being discussed at the water cooler. Continuous Improvement expert Courtney Dvorak said, "The talk at the water cooler is not reflective of the data we get in the employee engagement data we receive."

Something is not right.

---

11   That's one of the primary reasons for strong communication across the enterprise—to wipe out rumors before they start.

So, let's refocus "engagement." It's time for employees to look *outward*.

Your employees are already assessing your organization. What if we turned their employee gaze *outward* and asked them what they thought of their organization's ability to achieve outcomes? What if hundreds of individual employees considered the capabilities of their *overall* organization? What if they systematically looked at organizational capability? What if they focused on the larger elements of organizational performance? What if they looked *out* instead of *in*? What if they looked at *"We"* instead of *"Me"*?

Figure 4. Comparison of perspectives: "Me" vs. "We"

People have an intuitive sense of the organization's collective power, even from their limited view of their department or team. They have a sense of how resilient, how capable, how effective, or how exceptional your organization is today. They collectively know whether an organization *has what it takes to succeed.*

It's time for a new metric: Moving beyond employee engagement to Organizational Engagement.

So: How to measure at the organizational level? How would we measure whether people believe their companies can control outcomes to accomplish their strategic plans? We need something different. *That's the goal of the research behind this book.*

The Bohn Organizational Engagement Scale [BOES]

Starting with a study of 22 organizations, I developed a fresh approach to organizational analysis—The [BOES] Bohn Organizational Engagement Scale, a thirty-item scale that provides a complete analysis of Organizational Engagement. I will continue to explain the elements of this tool as the book unfolds, but it is critical to understand very early in the book that Organizational Engagement is a strategic concept for transforming organizations that goes beyond Employee Engagement.

Organizational Engagement: Moving beyond Employee Engagement

► **DEFINITION: Organizational Engagement is the level of motivation activated by employee perceptions of their organization's ability to achieve outcomes.**

There is a dramatic difference between **Employee Engagement** and **Organizational Engagement:** "Me" vs. "We." This is the critical distinction between the two approaches.

Chart 1.

Differences between Employee Engagement and Organizational Engagement

ME   WE

Employee Engagement Focused on	Organization Engagement Focused on
… exclusively on what employees derive from the organization	…what the organization derives from all employees working together
… individual motivation – what's in it for me?	…organizational level motivation – what's in it for us?
… 'local' issues such as environment, pay and benefits	…organizational level outputs such as customer satisfaction, product quality, and leader effectiveness across groups.
… the leader the individual works with each day	…how all leaders work together across the enterprise each day and throughout the year

What are the benefits of analyzing at the organizational level?

What are the benefits of approaching transformation through organizational level engagement? Why would an executive team want to switch from employee engagement to the organizational level? Specifically, *Organizational Engagement has the power to dramatically influence the enterprise in ways that cannot be achieved by EE.* What's the value of measuring at the organizational level? Measuring Organizational Engagement is a critical step toward determining if the organization has the power to manage outcomes.

Gathering data at the organizational level leads to organizational transformation. Research shows that "aggregated employee attitudes are related to organizational performance."[12] Think about that for just a minute: "aggregated employee attitudes" means everyone in the company is *already* thinking about organizational capability. As one journal article concludes, "Our results ... suggest that models that draw the causal arrows from employee attitudes to performance at the organizational level of analysis are at best too simplistic and at worst wrong."[13] In other words, the idea that employee morale creates organizational performance may be a bit presumptuous.

Consider the following critical questions:

1. Do your employees believe that the organization knows where it's going?

2. Do they believe members of the organization can work together to achieve outcomes?

3. Do they know what's going on through effective communication?

4. Is the organization strong enough to sail through difficult seas during times of trouble?

5. Do they believe your leadership can get things done?

6. Are they sure your organization rewards good work?

Do we have what it takes to win?

Organizational engagement provides companies with an analysis that will help them diagnose root cause problems to strengthen their organization for change. Asking (and trusting) employees to look *outward* and evaluate the strength of their organization is a revolutionary approach to organizational development whose time has come. The employees' collective view gives leaders a true answer to the question: *Do **we** have what it takes?* It is built around six basic yet critical elements of organizational behavior.

12　Schneider, Hanges, Smith, Salvaggio, (2003). "Which comes first, employees' attitudes or organizational and financial performance?" *Journal of Applied Psychology*, 88 (5), 836-851.

13　Ibid., 846.

Organization engagement analysis — the six elements

1. **Clarity of Mission:** Do we have confidence in where the organization is going?

2. **Cohesion:** Can we work together to achieve mission outcomes?

3. **Communication Effectiveness:** How well does the organization distribute critical information?

4. **Resilience:** Can we stay the course when times get tough?

5. **Leader Commitment:** Are our leaders capable of effectively achieving mission outcomes?

6. **Consequences/Accountability:** Are people rewarded and recognized fairly?

Figure 5. The Six Elements of Organizational Engagement

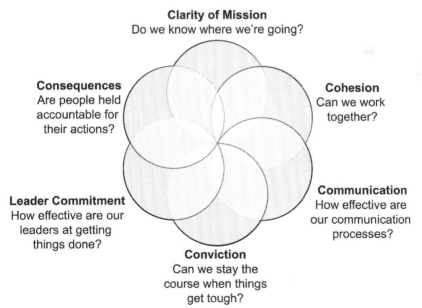

These six elements are interrelated, and although they can be treated separately based on priority, they mutually influence one another.

The Latest Twist in Employee Engagement: "The Employee Experience"

It is interesting that a recent article in *Forbes* asks, "What is the employee experience?"[14] Multiple answers are given, but the sense of a holistic look at organizational capability is missing. The fact is that the real "employee experience" is built on how employees evaluate the performance of the overall organization. It's what they're talking about at the water cooler. Yet we've turned it into yet a *new* buzzword—"the employee experience." Yet, if an organization cannot survive, it cannot provide *any* employee experience.

Here is a recent description of the "employee experience": "Growth and development, Feedback and coaching, Recognition and appreciation, Leadership, Communication, Camaraderie and Collaboration, Contributions, Trust and respect, Empowerment, Success.[15]

But what's missing?

The factors listed above are what an employee "experiences" every day (and very focused on the individual). And yet, the employee experience isn't just these things. This list is missing the critical fact that employees *know* whether their company has holistic operational thinking, wherewithal, and capacity required *to bring about* an "employee experience." What organizational behaviors create the employee experience? And how do leaders know which of those behaviors is having the most impact on the "employee experience"?

Organizational Engagement is a collective assessment of the entire organization's capability to shape an employee experience. Organizational Engagement is the employee evaluation of enterprise effectiveness including funding, leadership motivation, and focus moving in the right direction to achieve organizational level goals. All of these ultimately fulfill employee needs and are the true "employee experience".

---

14   https://www.forbes.com/sites/forbescoachescouncil/2019/02/01/what-exactly-is-the-employee-experience/#200a3ad54dbf "What Exactly Is the Employee Experience?"; Annette Franz Forbes Council Forbes Coaches Council, CommunityVoice.
15   Ibid.

What are the things that employees want most in the workplace?

People want to be excited about the direction of the company. People want to know their company has focus and a clear direction[16]. *They want to have confidence in the organization.* "My company is effectively managed and well run."[17] Employees need to feel they work for a well-led organization that is heading in a positive direction.[18]

All of these things are managed at the enterprise level.

What makes an employee want to *leave* an organization?

Top talent leaves an organization when they're badly managed and the organization is confusing and uninspiring.[19] People want to know that at the organizational level, the enterprise is moving in a clear and intentional direction. Employees want to know how they fit into organizational direction. **Ultimately, if the organization is moving forward with purpose, it can fulfill the needs of individual employees! It can create an incredible "employee experience".**

Bottom line: To create transformation and provide an incredible employee experience, organizations need an analytical approach that focuses on organizational level effectiveness beyond the individual employee.

That approach is Organizational Engagement.

16   http://www.workplacedynamics.com/blog/great-workplaces/the-2-things-employees-most-want-in-the-workplace/

17   Alan Church, *OD Practitioner*, (2013), 45, 2.

18   Hay Group, "Preparing for Take Off," White Paper.

19   Erika Andersen, "Why Top Talent Leaves: Top 10 Reasons Boiled Down to 1," *Forbes*.

Transfer Industries—
"There has to be a better way."

After the meeting with HR and the CEO, Engineering Director Bill Smith slowly walked down the hall toward his office. A couple of his team members stuck their heads out of the cubicles and offices.

"How'd it go?" asked Stephanie Broksher, a sharp engineer with multiple patents. "Any updates?"

"It's time for the Employee Engagement survey again—you guys all know the drill." Bill turned toward his desk, embarrassed to elaborate any further. Collective sighs and a few light chuckles rolled across the room. People went back to work on their PCs. "Business as usual," remarked one worker. "Same old garbage," quipped another.

Bill felt a red blush creep onto his face and his pulse quickened. He did not like being part of something he didn't really believe in, but he was a good corporate soldier who would fulfill his duty.

Stephanie walked over to Bill's office. "You know, I keep wondering why they do this every year. We get the same results and do the same things."

Bill tilted his head, lightly acknowledging her statement. As a good corporate leader, he wasn't about to get into criticizing executive leadership decisions. But he kept thinking, *There has to be a better way to measure.*

And he was right.

Chapter 2

It's Time to Move Beyond Employee Engagement

▶ **Employee Engagement has been around for decades and is still the predominant method of organizational analysis.**

▶ **Employee Experience is the latest trend in management, yet it misses a key element of organizational performance.**

▶ **A review of common methods for organizational analysis.**

▶ **It is time for HR to gain the organizational leverage it has been seeking.**

"Managers have to hound their leaders to hound their people to take the survey. If people believed in the value of employee engagement, they would take the survey naturally."

—*Courtney Dvorak, Continuous Improvement Expert*

"We took pulse surveys for four years and could not move the needle".

—*Executive leader Tom Lowery*

"If you want to be honest with employees, start by asking what they think of their company's survey process and whether they expect big changes from the next survey."

—*Jim Smith, LinkedIn*

Employee Engagement

Measuring employee engagement has been an organizational obsession for the past two decades. Yet using employee engagement surveys to assess the motivational level of employees, their satisfaction with their supervisor, and their perceived level of organizational support has a fundamental flaw. *They are one-sided and focused exclusively on the employee.* Employee engagement surveys focus *exclusively on the viewpoint of an individual—their internal world and perspective.* Yet employees inhabit a wider world called an organization. They do not act on their own.

At the risk of sounding like an OD (Organization Development) heretic, employee engagement is a *very narrow view of the universe*. When employees respond to EE questions, they will gravitate toward what is most comfortable to them, what most meets *their needs, not necessarily the needs of the organization*. What is good for one employee may be detrimental to many others. Yet we persist in using employee engagement as the predominant tool for organizational diagnosis.[20] It is a very me-focused approach, limited in its effectiveness.

Measuring employee engagement may not serve the interests of the corporation.

"One problem that companies often stumble over when using engagement measures is that different definitions of the term abound. The European version, for example, associated with Schaufeli, emphasizes the idea of "vigor,"[21] a term not used in other versions of engagement surveys. Consultants also tend to use different definitions from their competitors, which contributes to the confusion. Gallup Consulting, for instance, says that engagement is pride, passion, and enthusiasm for work. Willis Towers Watson defines it as "employees' willingness and ability to contribute to company success." One of the most widely cited pieces of engagement literature defines it differently still, as "the individual's involvement and satisfaction with as well as enthusiasm for work. The predicament is when an employer wants to find out, say, how hard employees are working, and the engagement survey it uses measures something else, such as pride in one's job or ability to contribute."[22]

---

20   As the book progresses, you will find recurring references to a book by Zinta S. Byrne, *Understanding Employee Engagement* (Routledge, 2015). At the time of writing, Byrne's book is the most recent, up-to-date, and thorough treatment of employee engagement, reviewing a significant amount of research in the literature. I have included her work in my analysis to assure the reader I have done my homework on employee engagement.

21   Schaufeli, W. B., Salanova, M., González-Romá, & Bakker, A. B. (2002). The measurement of engagement and burnout: A two sample confirmatory factor analytic approach. *Journal of Happiness Studies, 3*(1), 71-92.

22   Peter Cappelli and Liat Eldor, "Measuring Engagement Goes Wrong," in *HBR*, May 17, 2019. (https://hbr.org/2019/05/where-measuring-engagement-goes-wrong)

The organization is really not about you!

"Mission, vision, core values and attainment of strategic initiatives, for me, define success at an organizational level."

—*Monte Pedersen*

Organizational researchers have confirmed that an organization is far more than the sum of its parts. But people still assume organizational success is the result of employee engagement. The truth is, the organizational level is far more important than the individual level of analysis. Researchers know it. Executives know it. Managers know it. Individual employees know it. And in their honest moments, HR knows it.

Consider the following comparison of survey approaches: questions focused on an individual viewpoint versus questions focused on group effectiveness. This is a bit academically thick, shall we say, but nonetheless important to our discussion:

"Questions about group capability elicit perspectives on the obstacles, constraints, and opportunities of a given social system more readily than do items asking individuals about their self-capability, which varies more as a function of *individual* (*as opposed to group*), differences."[23]

Cutting through the academese, what this means is survey questions about the ability of a *group* to manage outcomes are **superior** to survey questions that focus on *individuals*. The literature on teamwork confirmed long ago that groups of people working together in organizations make the real difference in organizational performance.

In fact, with the pace of change and increased volume of organizational work, it is likely that the importance of group effectiveness will *escalate* in the future. Yet, most organizational surveys conducted today continue to focus exclusively on the view of an individual employee.

---

23   Goddard, R., Hoy, W. & Hoy, A. (2004). "Collective efficacy beliefs: theoretical developments, empirical evidence and future directions" in *Educational Researcher,* 33, (3), 3-13.

So let's take a very practical look at "The Employee Experience."

At one time (decades ago), there was coffee. One kind of coffee— maybe add sugar or cream. That was it. Some of it was horrible coffee from vending machines. Then came boutique coffee shops that added new, exciting drinks like macchiatos, mochas, doppias, flavored coffees, and so forth. Now we're at the level of oat milk with no end of variation in sight. Ordering coffee today is like a chemistry chart, and possibly more complex than a dinner at a five-star restaurant. Coffee is a very "individual" thing. We agree. I personally like the Sumatra blends.

The point is this: organizations are like coffee shops, forever in search of something new for the individual that will be the answer to organizational issues.

Employee engagement fades, employee experience rises

With the slow demise of employee engagement, a new shining star of organizational behavior is on the horizon called "The Employee Experience." It's simply engagement repackaged and rebranded for the sake of marketing. Businesspeople are always looking for the holy grail of employee satisfaction—maybe this is it! From what I've researched, The Employee Experience is a combination of (1) a website for customized training (yet few folks really like online learning) and (2) customized coaching and a (3) "fun" atmosphere, along with (4) explaining how employees fit into the greater scheme of the organization (*I like that one, btw*). Clearly there are other elements of the employee experience, but these components are mentioned most frequently.

Here's my reflection on why the Employee Experience will have its own endpoint in a relatively short time:

1. The Employee Experience is like a company newsletter—fun at first but difficult to maintain. Employees will eventually see through the perks and insincerity.

2. Because it is driven by individual interests, the Employee Experience tends to splinter people into smaller groups, driving us farther apart rather than bringing us together. It is individually focused, catering to a chronic need for self-satisfaction, when in fact, organizations need people to *work together.*

3. The Employee Experience is an infinite quest for fun in a place called... well... work! Fun gets old and boring very quickly, requiring companies to dream up new "fun" stuff, *ad infinitum.* (The company gym is now a foregone expectation – years ago it was the new thing."

4. Organizations cannot be like coffee shops catering to individual tastes because people join and leave companies. Work all you like to please one individual only to find out they are leaving tomorrow (this also happens with intense leadership development programming). You've wasted your time, and your organization has suffered a setback in the process.

5. One person's meat is another person's poison. I like some of the offerings at the coffee shop, but I'm not a big fan of other things on the menu. As you work hard to please me and my wants, you may be alienating someone else. Focus instead on the good of the organization—make it great—make its reputation great. People like to be part of a winning team. People want to be part of something bigger than themselves.

6. The prevailing social ethos today is individualism in a world that says it needs more collective effort. Yet organizations are not built around individuals and individual needs. They are built for the sake of maintaining a brand or an enterprise across geographies, markets, and time.

A great employee experience is the local manager and organizational reputation.

The local manager *is* the employee experience for most people.

The local manager is either a coach, guide, and advisor, or a difficult and demanding person who makes life miserable. No amount of employee experience is going to make up for a bad manager. Reams of research point to the local manager as the employee experience. *The local manager plays a key role in organizational engagement and will be discussed in detail further in this book.*[24]

Organizational achievements attract the best.

People like working for an organization that gives them a sense of accomplishment. Leaders should make that the goal. Make big things happen in the organization. People will stay with an organization that is well run and achieves big things and shares the praise and the profit.

But we're not finished yet! Enter "Work Engagement"

The term *Work Engagement* is defined as "a positive, fulfilling, work-related state-of-mind that is characterized by vigor, dedication, and absorption".[25] **Vigor** refers to high levels of energy, **dedication** refers to a sense of commitment, and **absorption** refers to being focused. The concept is very *me*, employee-focused, don't you think? A deeper question to ask is, "What organizational processes activate vigor, dedication, and absorption?" It cannot simply be the motivation of an individual employee. There is something bigger that activates motivational energy. Think about companies that have acquired (and sometimes lost) powerful reputations throughout the years: IBM, GE, 3M, Apple. Their employees were proud to work for such high-caliber organizations with internationally known reputations for innovation, achievement and global influence.

Work engagement, employee engagement, and employee experience are all focused on the individual*, not the enterprise they work for.* Buzzwords and catchphrases are fun and interesting, but they do not bring about increased organizational performance.

---

24   My LINKED IN post on this subject received over 25,000 responses https://www.linkedin.com/pulse/your-boss-90-employee-experience-nothing-else-comes-jim-bohn-ph-d-/
25   Schaufeli, Salanova, Gonzalez-Roma and Bakker, 2002.

Here's what we know: The latest management fads will not transform an organization!

We must always be wary of the latest "thing" in management practice, my readers. Better to focus on those behaviors that have made a difference over time and leave the fads to those who want buzzwords instead of real results.

Fads happen because business books get written that intrigue executives into thinking the Holy Grail of organizational performance has been found. Concepts like "The Employee Experience" and "Work Engagement" are two fads aimed at customizing an experience for employees with the hope of acquiring and retaining the best employees. The concept of customer satisfaction went through a period of infinite customization a few decades back, constantly refining markets to satisfy individual customers—it still goes on today. Some companies were able to keep up with constant refinement. But others went out of business because they could not adapt to mass customization.

Methods organizations have turned to for improved performance

Management performance fads have been around quite awhile. Organizations have been on a quest for the silver bullet for at least three decades. For example, Bolman and Deal asserted in 1992 that "Peak performance emerges as a team discovers its soul."[26] While that description is intriguing, it leaves us asking, "What exactly is the soul of a team?" In a similar vein in 1999, James Lucas wrote *The Passionate Organization: Igniting the Fire of Employee Commitment.* He said that "the most important measurement in any organization is morale, the level of positive (or negative) passion."[27] He continued, "Give us passion and we will burn up the speedway. We will learn new stuff, blurt it out in our excitement, and find whole new things to learn about that we hadn't even thought about yesterday. And we will create new ways to learn and teach, new ways to think, new ways to find joy in the journey."[28] While we sense emotional force behind these statements, we are left wondering how this approach could create powerful, sustained, intentional actions. And although both of those concepts inspired a group of readers who picked up books in airports, *they have not stood the test of time* to become standard methods for organizational improvement. We don't hear about these fads anymore. What once sold books is now passé.

---

26   Bolman, L., & Deal, T. (1992) "What makes a team work?" *Organizational Dynamics, 21*(2), 34-44. 44
27   p. 24
28   p. 145

Employee Engagement remains the predominant approach to organizational analysis

Zinta Byrne cites the following elements as "Drivers of Employee Engagement":

1. Meaningfulness

2. Alignment

3. Relationships

4. Communication

5. The Job Itself

6. Personal (voice, feedback, benefits)

7. Good Leadership[29]

Except for "Alignment," each of these drivers focuses on the experience of the *individual* employee. This list misses the critical element of organizational effectiveness. Here's why: the current state of organizational analysis is continually focused on *individual employee-level responses,* not the organizational level. Employee Engagement has been a focus of organizations for more than two decades. But it is outdated. Organizations have seen some change with EE, but we all know that for the past few years, overall Employee Engagement metrics have remained the same. In their 2017 report on the American workplace, Gallup acknowledges very little movement (a few percentage points) in the level of engaged employees.[30] Employees have become accustomed to the survey questions and know how to do an "end run" around the system. And leaders may not be all that enthusiastic about employee engagement anymore.

---

29 Byrne p. 74
30 Gallup, 2017 Report p. 179, 20122016

Reasons leaders may not be "engaged" in employee engagement

1. Leaders may *assume* they know the definition of engagement, but do not understand the concept.

2. Employee engagement is just another program to manage.

3. It's a check-the-box activity.

4. It's HR's job to manage.

5. Leaders may be insulated from the real results.

6. Leaders are rarely held accountable for employee engagement results.

7. Leaders may disregard the results because they're not truly interested.

8. Leaders may disregard the results because they may consider employee concerns to be just another "suggestion box."

9. Leaders don't want to hear about employee concerns on a wide variety of subjects.

10. Leaders may not even know how employees truly feel about the survey and feedback process.

11. Executives may not know that employees are *inoculated* against the process.

12. "Nothing has changed since the last time we took the last survey."

13. It seems like another management fad or flavor-of-the-day.

In short, leaders may not believe it works and they want to invest their money in things that yield ROI.

Formal Organization Development (OD) methods commonly used for Organizational Analysis

We've looked at the fads, but there are some fine formal instruments that historically have been used to assess organizations. Before we launch into the construct of Organizational Engagement, let's conduct some due diligence. Existing instruments measure various components of organizational performance. Here are several famous approaches to organizational analysis that have been used within recent decades (see Appendix B for a fuller treatment of each).

Construct	Authors	Approach
Organizational Culture[31]	Multiple	Interviews, surveys, consultant tools.
OCAI Instrument	Robert E. Quinn, Kim S. Cameron (1999, 2011)	Employee analysis through survey tools. Goal is to move organization to different approach over time.
Organization-Based Self-Esteem	Pierce, Jon & Gardner, Donald & L. Cummings, L & Dunham, Randall (1989)	An individual's view of how the organization helps them feel good about themselves.
Organizational Commitment	Eby, Lillian & M. Freeman, Deena & C. Rush, Michael & Lance, Chuck (1999)	An Individual viewpoint of organizational process and strategy.
Organizational Climate	Pierce, Jon & Gardner, Donald & L. Cummings, L & Dunham, Randall (1989)	An individual's view of how comfortable the organization makes them.
Organizational Citizenship	Organ (1990); Lee, K., & Allen, N. J. (2002)	An individual's view of how the organization can activate personal motivation to go beyond the call of duty.
Perceived Organizational Support	Eisenberger (1999)	An individual's view of how the organization helps them.
Organizational Health	Lencioni (2012)	Leadership team process—not the organizational level
Balanced Scorecard	Norton and Kaplan (1996)	Four aspects of organizational performance
Employee Engagement	Harter, et al. (2002)	An individual's view of how the organization helps them.

31   "No research today offers a single-point confirmation or solid evidence providing the type of comprehensive and complex culture… that will ensure (a) and engaged workforce or (b) a competitive advantage." (Byrne, 139)

| Description | **Chart 2. Methods of Organizational Analysis** |

Culture is "the glue that binds an organization together.... It is the collection of values, beliefs, symbols, and norms the organization follows that define what it is and how it does business each and every day." (SHRM, Fornal, 2002)

Emphasizes culture types within different organizations, including Dominant Archetypes of Clan Culture, Adhocracy Culture, Market Culture, and Hierarchy Culture

Focused on how an individual employee feels about themselves in an organization. In other words, how does participation in a specific organization contribute to one's self-esteem?

"An individual's attitude towards the organization, consisting of a strong belief in, and acceptance of, an organization's goals, willingness to exert considerable effort on behalf of the organization and a strong desire to maintain membership in the organization."

"Climate is the psychological process that mediates the relationships between the work environment (conceived as an objective set of organizational policies, practices, and procedures) and work-related attitudes and behaviors."

Organizational citizenship behaviors include such things as "helping others with their jobs, volunteering for additional work, and supporting organizational objectives."

How the organization supports the individual

Its focus is primarily on the leadership team cohesion and clarity of mission.

Financial, Organizational Stakeholder, Customer, Internal Process

Q12 process to assess employee engagement

Summary of the approaches: *Their primary focus in the organization is the individual.*

Beyond these formal instruments are the more popular tools like DiSC, Myers-Briggs, Strengths-Finder, and others with varying levels of reliability. All of them are, again, focused on the *individual*. While these approaches have some value at the line level for developing awareness of strengths and weaknesses, they do not address the issues that make dramatic organizational change. They ask, in short, "what is the organization **doing for me,** so I may do something to benefit it?" Byrne writes that "Engagement in organizations looks like employees loving their jobs."[32] *That's not a bad thing, but again, it is the individual's view of their situation within the organization.*

But managers view things differently.

Managers take a different view of what it takes to make an organization tick. For example, here are some quotes I've heard from managers seeking to improve their organizations.

They say they want: "Missional focus. Passionate, energized staff, working together."

"Making sure people understand strategy."

"Resilience."

"The biggest challenge is getting people focused/aligned."

"Creating North Star Vision."

"You can move mountains when you have people aligned."

Notice that each of these simple statements exceeds the vision and experience of an *individual* employee. It's about what makes an organization tick

Employees want to know if their organization *has what it takes*.

The following quote is a bit academic, but critical to understanding why the group viewpoint is more important than the individual viewpoint.

Shamir (1990) states:

"In the case of collective tasks whose accomplishment depends

---

32   Byrne, 21

on collective efforts, it is not rational to make an effort if collective efficacy (the ability to accomplish outcomes) is perceived to be low, because no matter how strong the perceived relationship between rewards and collective accomplishments, the chances of such accomplishment and therefore of obtaining rewards, are perceived to be low. *Hence, a cognitive calculative formulation of collectivistic motivation must include the individual's subjective probability that the collective efforts will result in collective (organizational, departmental, or team) accomplishment."*[33]

In other words, people in organizations have a sense of whether the organization has what it takes to survive and thrive and that assessment drives employee effort. Since that is true - it's time to move beyond employee engagement to ***organizational engagement.***

Finally, HR has been seeking a "seat at the table" for some time, but still needs a methodology that makes sense to executive leadership.

Even with all the tools and techniques listed above, HR has often been stymied in its pursuit of a methodology that can create dramatic, transformative change, because the individual level is not the answer. Employee level concerns are inadequate for organizational analysis and improvement and may cause more trouble than they're worth. Consider this quote:

Sometimes engagement programs cause more trouble than they resolve.

"What engagement programs actually do, according to Cy Wakeman, author of *noego*, is "inflate expectations and sow unhappiness, leaving employees unprepared to adapt to even minor changes necessary to the organization's survival. Rather than driving performance and creating efficiencies, these programs fuel entitlement and drama, costing millions in time and profit."

"Employee, member and even customer engagement, in theory, are wonderful for any business to focus on. But, they're practically useless – unless you're aligning these with your organization's purpose and strategy. The problem is that so many leaders have become so captivated by the need for engagement that they are forgetting to ask why it matters."
—George Brandt, *Forbes*, 9/18/2013

---

33   Shamir 1990, 5.

So, the big questions remain...

With all the organizational development work done for decades using instruments that have been developed to analyze organizations, fundamental questions remain:

1. **How does an organization achieve strategic outcomes?**

2. **What makes an organization tick?**

3. **What is happening at the *organizational level* to bring about the accomplishments, completed projects, and strategic achievements the organization desires?**

The answer to these questions lies *not within the individual employee, but at the Organizational Level.*

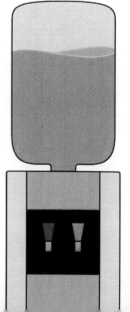

Transfer Industries:

"Organizations get sick, just like people, and they need to be diagnosed."

"I've been around here a long time," Bill said as he walked into Dale Argent's office, "and we've used employee engagement forever. But you know and I know that it's about more than employee discussions and surveys. Organizations are made of a variety of people, projects, initiatives, and strategies. One person can't change that—it's the whole company working together that makes things happen. We're fooling ourselves if we think an employee survey focused on individuals is going to make our organization better."

"I gotta admit you're right, Bill," Dale responded, "and, candidly, I've seen organizational level crises that go well beyond the individual. Things go wrong at the organizational level and those things impact everyone. It's a vicious cycle."

"What do you mean, organizational-level crises?" Bill asked intently.

"An organization can have organizational-level distress; sicknesses that are well beyond any individual's ability to correct."

Bill looked at Dale intently, scratching his head. "I have never thought of it that way. We're all so buried in our day-to-day activities, we can't really see what's going on at the higher level of complexity."

"Exactly," Dale replied. "Organizations get sick like people—and it takes serious leadership to sort it out and change it."

Bill responded, "But first you'd have to evaluate at the organizational level to truly diagnose the distress."

Dale smiled. "Yes, that's exactly what you'd need to do."

And that's exactly what needs to be done.

Chapter 3:

Chronic Organizational Problems and Business Distresses

- ▶ **Chronic business problems must be diagnosed at the organizational level.**
- ▶ **Businesses struggle at the organizational level.**
- ▶ **Six common organizational level distresses.**

Organizational behavior is far more complex than most popular leadership literature would have us believe. Issues of employee motivation, organizational structure, leadership style, alignment of organizational skills with organizational desires increase levels of organizational complexity and interrelated dynamics. Ever wonder what that leads to? Sometimes employees are confused, sometimes they're angry, sometimes they're bewildered, and sometimes they're looking for the door. When people become disillusioned, they become disengaged. We hear a lot about employee engagement, but not a whole lot about employee disengagement. Yet organizations suffer from disengagement in many ways.

Some time back, I saw this LinkedIn post about employee *disengagement.* It raised a serious question: **"Are all forms of disengagement the same?" The author, Dr. Clayton, enumerated the forms of disengagement.**

Are all forms of disengagement the same?

Overwhelmed disengagement: feeling over-stretched, under-appreciated, anxious, or risking burnout

Critical disengagement: skeptical, ironic, and pragmatic, but (mis)perceived as cynicism, mockery, and negativity by mainstream management thought

Bored disengagement: unchallenged by the work one has to do, resulting in apathy

Resistant disengagement: a conscious refusal to engage with novel or different ways and methods of working

Angry disengagement: furious at the way in which management has acted and actively sabotaging in response

Fatigued disengagement: burnt out by faddish changes and interventions that cause extra work without ever seriously addressing fundamental issues

Fearful disengagement: Fear of job security in uncertain times and becoming redundant due to lack of relevant skills (and ageism)."[34]

The issues Dr. Clayton describes above have a dramatic impact on organizational performance, and employees discuss these forms of disengagement at the water cooler. They show (1) that employee disengagement can emerge in a variety of personal behaviors, (2) that cynicism in the ranks fuels disengagement, and (3) that organizational insecurities can cause employee disengagement. Those insecurities are a result of organizational-level ineffectiveness that can only be diagnosed at the organizational level.

---

34   Clayton, R. (2019, January 20). Posts. LinkedIn page. Retrieved from https://www.linkedin.com/feed/update/urn:li:activity:6493032987150639104

Where does organizational-level ineffectiveness start?

Organizational ineffectiveness is all around us, often in the most mundane, unexciting and sometimes even boring places, but it exists everywhere. Here are a few examples:

- Organizations are often **siloed**. That is, departments focus on their own needs to the exclusion of—and sometimes to the detriment of—the success of others. This behavior has a negative impact on organizational output. As Monte Pedersen notes: "This is a big one, and especially prevalent in large matrix-based organizations. When there is no clarity at the top (leaders leading with well-defined initiatives and goals and commitment from the team), nothing beyond the personal or departmental gets accomplished. When there is no buy-in and commitment, it becomes everyone for themselves."[35]

- Managers find it **difficult to focus** because of excessive (and sometimes *conflicting*) initiatives.

- People are often **uncertain** about how their work fits into organizational success, exacerbating ineffectiveness and increasing social loafing.

- **Leaders use sound bites**—quick statements as they pass in a hallway—to communicate, often leading to confusion.

- Ineffective projects and programs are **left in place**, draining precious organizational time and energy (breathing dinosaurs).

What *behaviors* contribute to organizational-level ineffectiveness?

1. People do not **communicate** effectively enough to provide data flow and make effective decisions.

2. People **do not work together** to solve problems or worse, they compete with each other, resulting in negative effects for the corporation.

3. People are unsure of their roles in supporting the organization's **mission**.

4. Incomplete or unnecessary projects absorb valuable **resources (also known as *escalated commitment*)**.

---

35   M. Pedersen, personal conversation.

5. The organization demonstrates poor levels of managerial **accountability**. Again, Monte Pedersen weighs in: "This is big, as leadership doesn't always have a 'follow up and through' mentality. We get what we tolerate, right? They believe they are 'micro-managing' or that they should only have to tell a manager something once. Lots of mixed signals happen here that often give team members 'cover' for poor performance."

6. **Ineffective leaders** remain in positions of authority, negatively influencing others, which has a domino effect on tens, even hundreds and thousands of people. "When the organization goes into the death spiral, ineffective leadership is what is usually driving it." —M. Pedersen

There's currently no effective way to measure and isolate these chronic, organization-wide issues, even though they have a massive impact on the performance and effectiveness of the overall organization. Let's take a close look at six types of organizational distress.

Business distress occurs at the organizational level

Organizational success goes beyond individual employee engagement. Employees know it. When organizations are not managed well, they develop sicknesses and distress that impact performance. Before we look deeper into Organizational Engagement, we need to think through stresses that impact the organization, *well beyond the information provided by Employee Engagement surveys.* Although anecdotes from employees may be indicative symptoms of organizational sickness and stress, these stresses cannot easily be detected at the employee level—they must be diagnosed at the *organizational level.*[36]

Enterprise distress is analogous to individual distress.

It is a fact that people can be neurotic, depressed, angry, distracted, insecure, or anxious. Individuals manifest psychological distress from frustrating daily symptoms to significant lifetime impairment. By analogy, organizations display strikingly similar forms of psychological distress. By using this analogy, as opposed to a more sugar-coated set of terms, leaders can take a fresh—perhaps hard—look at the realities facing their organizations, allowing them to take corrective action. Leaders are the "organizational physicians" who must take action to improve their "patients."

---

36   Every employee is going to have their own experience and evaluate the corporation through their own lens of success or achievement. It is only the collective analysis of an organization that tells the true story. One person speaking loudly because of a perceived injustice is one thing; 50–60 people saying the same thing is a completely different matter.

> **Disclaimer:** This chapter is in no way intended to demean the serious suffering of individuals whose lives have been disrupted by emotional/cognitive diseases and disorders. I am empathetic to their plight. The distress analogy is powerful and helpful for leaders seeking to repair organizational dysfunction. The purpose of this chapter is to help and not harm.

Organizational distress

Based on my four decades of experience as a leader, practitioner, researcher/educator, and, most importantly, a social scientist who lived in the field and *did* the work of leading teams, I have observed several recurring forms of organizational distress.

In the current economic climate of exceptionally low unemployment, these distresses can have a dramatic impact on retention and turnover. (In a high unemployment economy, team members disengage and stay). Leaders do well to consider whether their organizations are on the cusp of these distresses. Analyzing organizational engagement helps leaders to see these issues and gives them a clear path for course correction. These distresses are listed in no particular order, though organizations could suffer from some or all of them at the same time.[37] Any of the following distresses impacts the true employee experience.

They are as follows:

I. **O.A.D.D.(Organizational Attention Deficit Disorder)**

II. **Recognition Anorexia—Forgetting what people have done**

III. **Organizational Co-Dependency**

IV. **Organizational Narcissism**

V. **Enterprise Anxiety Disorder**

VI. **Organizational Depression**

---

37   There are others that extend beyond the space available for this book. See my article on LinkedIn: https://www.linkedin.com/pulse/eight-forms-organizational-distress-symptoms-impact-jim-bohn-ph-d-/

I. O.A.D.D. (Organizational Attention Deficit Disorder)

Symptoms: When an organization has O.A.D.D., people have so many projects on their plate they can't keep up. People are asked to take on more and more and more before they have finished current work, causing indecision. O.A.D.D. is like schizophrenia, which comes from *schizein* and *phren*—two Greek words—meaning, literally, a split mind. Employee uncertainty, team infighting, and ineffective, diluted distribution of resources are symptoms of this organizational distress.

Causes of O.A.D.D.:

1. Ineffective strategy

2. Unfocused leadership: their inability to say no to the latest shiny object

3. Competition between upper-level leaders for turf—Leadership ego gets in the way of a clear path. This form of organizational distress can be caused by leadership intentionally going in different directions due to competing ego goals and strategies.

4. No "air-traffic controller" or project management office (PMO) at the executive level assessing the number of new programs being generated and sent to front-line managers. This is a big factor in O.A.D.D.

5. Project overload from excessive organizational initiatives—HR, Legal, Operations, or Product Development, for example, sends an organization into O.A.D.D by burdening people with too much at one time.

6. Strategic uncertainty. Too many cooks in the kitchen setting direction—generally the effect of a dysfunctional executive team.

Impact: Because of **O.A.D.D.**, people lose focus and become indecisive. Energy is diluted and projects are performed ineffectively. People experience cognitive overload (yes, this is a real thing!) and burnout. Organizations experience customer complaints and profit loss. **Worst of all, precious human motivation is expended without effect.**

II. Recognition Anorexia — Forgetting what people have done

I once spoke at a conference and asked a large group of managers why they didn't recognize people. One guy shouted out: "We don't need to do that stuff, we pay them for what they do." This is not an uncommon sentiment from leaders I have met in my travels.

Organizations talk a lot about recognition but do very little recognizing because they're worried "people will slow down or stop working because we gave them recognition." The social science data simply shows that that's false. Recognition energizes people because it indicates they've accomplished something.

Symptoms: Managers rarely acknowledge people for work well done. Performance reviews do not cite accomplishment. People feel like their work does not matter. Performance feedback does not acknowledge achievement. Management has selective memory loss impacting people who have achieved much but have been recognized for little. Busy organizations often forget to recognize simply due to the speed of the operation—things are moving too quickly.

Causes:

1. Inaccurate fear that recognition will lead to a slowing down of the workforce.

2. Recognition takes effort that managers may choose to avoid, "because we have real work to do."

3. Fear that recognition will be unjust, *so no one gets recognized.*

Impact: The very thing people need to thrive in the workplace (validation through recognition) is being withheld from them. People spend a third of their lifetimes in the workplace, and *the workplace may be the only place they get validation.* People who have worked hard will sense inequity and injustice leading to turnover, or worse, they will stay and do the minimum until they can find another job.

When achievements go unnoticed or unrecognized, people lose the desire to achieve more. They even lose the belief that they **can** achieve more. The concept is called *"learned helplessness."* They will also feel they have been treated unfairly and are likely to remember this injustice for many years.

A strange secondary cause of recognition anorexia: *Managers that are jealous of underlings who are rising stars are cautious about bragging too much.*

III. Organizational Co-Dependency: The Consultant

Symptoms: In organizations with co-dependency, consultants have become a crutch, with the consultant as a facilitator for understanding all the problems within a company, yet rarely if ever resolving them. In some cases, consultants manage whole parts of the business.

Causes:

1. Executive relationships or hires from a former consulting company

2. Executive insecurity about organizational direction

3. Excessive reliance on outside sources of information

4. Overreliance on comparisons with other "benchmark" companies served by the consultant

Impact: Executives spend excessive amounts of money and time deferring to outside consultants, asking for advice and direction.[38] Internal experts feel disrespected and disengage. Employees are left to implement or pick up the pieces after the consultants leave.

IV. Organizational Narcissism

Symptoms: This is also known as hubris. The business is losing ground, but the executives are *so absorbed in their past achievements* that they cannot see how fast the future is hurtling toward them. These leaders have radical blind spots. They believe they can still maneuver their business quickly as if the *Exxon Valdez* could be turned like a sailboat.

This distress is especially common among self-made entrepreneurs who have been wildly successful for decades but have lost sight of what is happening around them as their business grows out of control. It is equally true for well-funded startups that cannot manage radical growth.

---

38   Consultants rarely live with the results of their recommendations, by the way. Ask the consultant whether they are willing to accept a percentage of the increased sales or profitability instead of their usual fees, and the relationship will change drastically.

Causes:

1. Overestimation of skills

2. Underestimation of market forces

3. Willful blindness to employee calls for action

4. Ignoring customer complaints

5. Leadership ego

Impact: Executives discover too late that they were wrong about their long-held assumptions that their business or product will endure forever. Employee turnover, loss of business, and customer complaints lead to a corporate death spiral.

V. Enterprise Anxiety Disorder

Symptoms: When Enterprise Anxiety Disorder takes hold, people in your company are unable to think clearly. They demonstrate frustration with each other and are sensitive to things that would normally not be an issue. They overreact or are paralyzed and unable to make decisions.

Causes:

1. Leaders who are unable to overcome loss of market share or product failure

2. Excessive products and services catering to opposing markets

3. Excessive growth in a short period of time

4. Failed organizational initiatives that are burning people out with no one willing to call out the failure

5. Poor product quality leading to customer complaints

6. Ineffectively managed downsizing

Impact: Anxiety eventually causes burnout and employee frustration leading to turnover. Organizations experience a loss of product quality. A devastating effect is the formation of cliques who support each other (but complain about other groups) during times of stress.

VI. Organizational Depression

Symptoms: People are listless and not generating new ideas. They are engaged in social loafing and *complaining more than getting the work done*. The sources of Organizational Depression vary, but the most likely issue is one of inconsistent leadership causing people to feel like their effort is wasted. They mark time and fold their arms, waiting for something significant to redirect the organization.

Causes:

1. Depression in individuals is anger turned inward because of injustice or frustration with a situation. This can be very true of organizations. When ineffective managers remain in place, the organization suffers from a despair of *ever getting things right*.

2. The ineffective use of employee time contributes to Organizational Depression. Employees want leadership to know: "Don't waste my time, and don't ask for my ideas if you're not going to use them."

3. The sources of Organizational Depression vary, but the most likely issue is inconsistent direction causing people to feel like their time and effort are wasted. Incompetent leaders are also a common source of Organizational Depression because people cannot alleviate the chronic and constant stress of someone making bad or inconsistent decisions with no follow-through. People know they are wasting their time (and lives!).

4. Ineffectively managed downsizing

Impact: People become cynical and lose interest in new strategies coming down from executives. Thus, they expend minimal effort on projects, and limit their personal initiative to try new things. Everything slows down and the company feels the impact.

Organizational Distress can happen to _any_ company.

Even the best organizations can become complacent, disordered, confused or have moments of chaos that become exceptionally stressful. Consider GE or Sears, for example. The world has seen organizations in various phases of distress that lead to collapse. Once distress is diagnosed, interventions from wise, caring, and *persistent* leaders are the answer. But a diagnosis comes first, and *that diagnosis **must** be at the **organizational level.***

Here are two critical points:

(1) Employee Engagement is not going to reveal (or resolve) these distresses.

(2) These distresses are part of the daily "employee experience," and no amount of perks is going to overcome the strain employees experience in these environments.

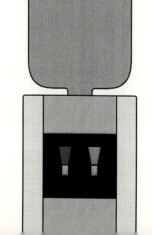

Transfer Industries:

"It's time to turn our awareness into action."

"You know, it's interesting," Dale continued. "All the engagement materials are focused on the individual employee—what an individual employee can do, but we both know that it is people working together that make the impact."

Bill answered, "That's right! *The things we accomplish together are what really matter.* I think about the big projects that include hundreds, even thousands, of our team members worldwide, and sometimes even though people leave those teams, the organization goes on. It's the organizational level that counts."

Dale continued, "The HR world has focused so much on the individual, we've lost sight of the whole purpose for evaluating our organization. We need to survive in the marketplace!"

Just then, Jennifer Stampleton knocked on Dale's office door and stepped inside. "Got a second?" she asked.

"Sure," Dale responded, wondering for a second if Jennifer heard his last statement. Thinking the conversation would be confidential, Bill got ready to leave.

"Please stay, Bill," Jennifer requested. "Your input is important, so I'm glad you're here."

"What's on your mind, Jennifer?" Dale asked.

"Well, I'm thinking there's a whole different way to look at how employees get 'engaged.'"

"What do you mean?"

"Well, think about it. People have a real sense of how we're doing as an organization. They know when we're succeeding, and they want to be part of a winning team. That sense of being part of something must surely activate motivation."

Bill smiled. "You're right, you know."

Jennifer focused her attention on him. "Go on."

"The people I hire tell me they want to be part of a winning operation. They come here to create something big, to be part of an organization famous for achievement. And when they hear about success in other parts of the organization, they get fired up. They're *engaged*!"

Jennifer said ,"It's time we took a hard look at the organizational level."

She did what all great executives do:
she turned her awareness into action.

Chapter 4:

It's time to rethink engagement

▶ **A significantly different approach is required to effectively transform organizations.**

▶ **Employee engagement is a measurement of individual motivation.**

▶ **Organizational analysis is required to solve organizational level problems.**

▶ **We need to move beyond employee engagement to organizational engagement**

Let's take a look at Employee engagement, *one last time.*

This chapter is brief, yet the voice is intentionally academic to show the origins of Employee Engagement (it came from the academy) and to demonstrate the need to move beyond it.

In an up-to-date analysis of employee engagement, researcher Zinta Byrne (2015) conducted a review of the literature and defined employee engagement as:

> "A moment-to-moment state of motivation, wherein one is psychologically present (in the moment) and psychologically aroused, is focused on and aligned with the goals of the job and organization and channels his or her emotional and cognitive self to transform work into meaningful and purposeful accomplishments".[39]

That's a mouthful, to say the least, but it demonstrates the complexity of trying to explain employee engagement[40]. One of the reasons employee engagement has challenges is because of how it is defined and managed academically and organizationally—there is no consistent definition. Ultimately, Byrne reminds us that employee engagement is about, well, the *employee*! While the employee is "focused on and aligned with the goals of the job and the organization," the employee is still channeling "his or her emotional and cognitive effort to transform work into meaningful and purposeful accomplishments." In short, the employee may

---

39 Byrne, 15
40 The construct of employee engagement has as many definitions as there are researchers.

be *engaged*, but in pursuit of personally meaningful accomplishments. There is no doubt those accomplishments have value, and it is critical that managers and leaders find ways to create the environments for people to use their "accomplishments" to achieve organizational ends. Yet a "meaningful accomplishment" for one person may contradict a "meaningful accomplishment" for another, thus minimizing the *organizational impact* of alignment. Making work meaningful to oneself is a laudable element of employee engagement but is missing organizational level focus.

Organizational focus is the missing piece

Byrne examines the research to show relationships between employee engagement and organizational citizenship, job satisfaction, "flow," and intrinsic motivation. [41] Ultimately, those constructs are also self-focused—how my work has value, how it creates meaning for me, and how my efforts matter to the organization. In short, these metrics are focused on the self. **Employee engagement is a measurement of an _individual experience_ in the context of the workplace.**

Global employee engagement is focused on the individual, not the organization.

Having been around since at least the early 2000s (Harter, Schmidt, and Hayes, 2002) employee engagement surveys have become a staple for most organizations worldwide using tools from KENEXA, Gallup, Towers-Watson, Deloitte, Hay Group, and other consulting firms.[42] The tools in use are focused on the *individual employee*. To understand a "meta-view"[43] of EE, the Global Employee Engagement Index[44] arrived at these four pillars of employee engagement (across 54 countries):

1. "A compelling company *culture* where *employees feel they fit in, are appreciated, and are proud of what the organization stands for and does.*

2. An optimal work *environment* where *employees are free to work and perform*, do what they are good at, and develop.

3. Exceptional *leaders* at the C-suite level who inspire confidence, keep up-to-date with current affairs and communicate.

4. Inspiring *immediate* managers that motivate, use employee feedback and are proficient in people management."

---

41 Mihaly Csikszentmihalyi, *Flow: The Psychology of Optimal Experience*
42 Aon Hewitt (2016). *2016 Trends in global employee engagement: Employee engagement is on the rise,* but volatility abounds. Deerfield, IL: Author.
43 Meta meaning a study of many studies.
44 Barends, A. (2016). *Global Employee Engagement Index* (vol. 3). Amsterdam: Effectory International, 13.

Number 1 tells us that *the organizational level matters*: "employees are… proud of what the organization stands for and does," and we learn something else: the C-suite inspires confidence across the enterprise—that's bigger than individual motivation.

Employee engagement has demonstrated some positive effects.

To be fair, employee engagement has demonstrated some positive correlations with organizational performance, customer satisfaction, and other metrics (although the actual definition and variables within employee engagement often vary between consulting firms).[45] Overall, the tool and concept are being used widely, yet many studies consistently show that 70% of people are NOT engaged, which dilutes executive enthusiasm for more engagement programs. The reasons for a lack of engagement are beyond the scope of this book, but research shows that employee engagement is not working to change organizations.

My view of "engagement" is taking part in the action—committing to something bigger than yourself.

From my perspective, engagement is being part of the action, committing energy and effort to *organizational* goals, for the sake of the organization and not just for employee self-satisfaction. Engagement is an *employee choice* to move out of the inertia of routine, to exert their attention, effort, and energy to achieve organizational success. That's engagement. In short, employees are motivated by an awareness of their organization's collective ability to produce financial outcomes and persevere in difficult business climates. As Byrne acknowledged, "Organizations that can provide a superordinate goal to which employees can connect and feel joined with others in achieving may result in employees finding meaning and ultimately engagement."[46]

People will expend effort toward something they believe in, something that they believe will succeed. I was once part of a team of fifty people who integrated a 256-million-dollar organization in an M&A (Merger and Acquisition). It was hard work, but in the end, we stood on a mountaintop of success. We had accomplished what many thought would be impossible. We were focused on a goal far bigger than ourselves.

We focused our talents, energy, and effort on the organizational level—not on ourselves.

---

45   These correlations have been argued against by such researchers as Jim Smith, who states that organizations that are well run are likely to have good engagement scores. Correlations are not cause and effect. Also see Byrne, Table 6.1, 115-20.

46   Byrne, 66.

Chapter 5

Organizational Engagement:
What you'd hear if your water cooler could talk

▶ **Definition: Organizational Engagement is the level of
employee motivation activated by employee perceptions
of their organization's ability to achieve outcomes.**

Moving out of inertia into momentum

People in your organization have a sense of "how things get done around here." We call that *culture*. Culture is people's sense of *what's going on* in their organization, so they can make decisions and do their work. Employees assess their culture to make sense of how the organization is performing in the marketplace. Employees have a perception of how likely it is that the organization will accomplish its goals.[47] Employee perceptions of an organization's ability to achieve goals activate (or deactivate) personal motivation. It happens at water coolers across the world (and smoking sheds, I'm told!).

Members of an organization intuitively know whether their organization has the capability to achieve desired strategic outcomes. People sense organizational ability every day as they (1) assess their leaders' confidence, (2) weigh the strategies the organization has developed, (3) perceive accountability for work quality, (4) evaluate the quality of communication shared, and (5) observe the way teams work together. All of those elements of organizational behavior reach far beyond an individual employee's influence.

What motivates employees to exert _sustained energy_ in pursuit of organizational goals?

Think about it: What causes individual employees to exert their energy toward organizational goals? What throws the switch in their personal motivational systems to say *I'm going to work, sacrifice, and persist for the organization*? That's organizational engagement. What gives

---

47   Bohn, 2010.

people a sense that their efforts will pay off and are worthwhile? What is needed at the organizational level to inspire individuals to bring about the accomplishments, completed projects, and strategic achievements desired by the organization? And what perceptions do employees experience that switch on motivational power to work hard on behalf of the organization? Hint: It is **not** employee engagement. It is something **much** bigger.

What does a highly engaged organization look like?

I recall one of my former leaders say that when he visited a field operation, "you could feel the *buzz* in the branch." In companies with high levels of Organizational Engagement, people function differently, work differently, and the outcomes are different than in those where organizational engagement is low. People cope differently and think differently, because they sense the collective power of their organization to accomplish collective goals.

Organizational Engagement is, at its root, a construct or *way of thinking*. A simple way to think about OE is that people who are highly engaged can persist in the face of obstacles. *Because they are confident in their organization's ability to achieve outcomes,* they have the drive to take on larger projects resulting in a track record of accomplishments.[48]

What activates organizational engagement?

People have a clear sense of what an organization must do to achieve strategic goals. **Individuals are motivated if:**

1. an organization is well-focused,
2. it works well together,
3. it is well led,
4. it communicates effectively,
5. it holds people accountable for work products and quality,
6. it has staying power in the face of obstacles.

---

48   Bandura, 1993

A look at the Social Science Roots of Organizational Engagement:

Collective Efficacy

Organizational Engagement is based on the social science construct of organizational efficacy—an organization's ability to control outcomes (which finds its roots in self-efficacy). The idea is simple: To perform effectively, groups need to believe they can control outcomes.[49] People hold a belief about a group's capabilities. In academic parlance, "Collective efficacy refers to an *individual's assessments of their group's collective ability to perform job-related behaviors*"[50] Here's the bottom line: **people know whether their group can get the job done.**

Let me anchor the concept a bit more. The famous social scientist Albert Bandura wrote: "Perceived collective efficacy will influence what people choose to do as a group, how much effort they put into it, and their staying power when group efforts fail to produce results"[51], and "Perceived collective efficacy is defined as a group's shared belief in its conjoint capabilities to organize and execute courses of action required to produce given levels of attainments"[52]. How does collective efficacy influence a group? "Belief of collective efficacy affects the sense of mission and purpose of a system, the strength of common commitment to what it seeks to achieve, how well its members work together to produce results, and the group's resilience in the face of difficulties."[53]

The point is this: *An organization's ability to achieve outcomes is founded on the collective employee view of an organization's capabilities. What employees believe about the organization activates or deactivates their motivation. It is the organizational level that counts.*

---

49   Shea, G. B., & Guzzo, R. A. (1987). Group effectiveness: What really matters? *Sloan Management Review, 28*(3), 25-31 p. 27
50   Riggs et al. (1994), 794.
51   Bandura. A. (1986). *Social foundations of thought and action.* Englewood Cliffs: Prentice Hall.
52   Bandura, 1997, p. 477
53   Bandura, 1997, p. 469

Organizational Engagement Defined

"Organizational Engagement is the level of motivation activated by employee perceptions of their organization's ability to achieve outcomes."

Organizational-level engagement is the employees' perception that an organization can achieve strategic objectives.. It is about more than one individual assessing organizational capabilities. *It is beyond employee level engagement, which is largely focused on the individual.*

With this analysis in mind, the Bohn Organizational Engagement Scale (BOES) was designed and validated to assess six elements of Organizational Engagement.[54] It is a thirty-item survey with detailed questions about:

> ▶ *innovation*: an organization's ability to generate new ideas
>
> ▶ *collaboration*: the cohesiveness of people working together
>
> ▶ *leader effectiveness*: the perception that leaders stay the course and get things done
>
> ▶ *accountability*: an organization's approach to justice and fairness
>
> ▶ *resilience*: an organization's ability to persist in the face of obstacles
>
> ▶ *communication*: the effectiveness of transmitting information to those who need it for decisions and direction.

Viewing the organization in totality: OE is the true Employee Experience

54 BOES has been translated into Spanish, French, Russian, Chinese, Japanese, Dutch, and Italian.

The "employee experience" is more than volleyball fields or a good cafeteria. The employee experience is an overall perception of the organization. Organizational engagement includes hiring, training, leadership, finance, workplace environment, mission, goals, departmental contributions, and communication. Organizational engagement encompasses the entirety of sales, marketing, production, distribution, HR, legal, manufacturing, engineering, and operations, all moving toward organizational achievement. Each of these functions by themselves contribute their part to overall organizational success. Although they can be judged in isolation, each is but a small part of overall organizational performance. For example, hiring may be fantastic, but leadership and communication may be atrocious, minimizing the effectiveness of good hiring practices.

When leaders assess the level of Organizational Engagement in their company, they consider their company's capacity to achieve outcomes, weighing the effectiveness of human energy, funding, and employee motivation to accomplish organizational goals. OE is an assessment of whether the enterprise will accomplish organizational strategies. It is a collective perception of how an organization works together to achieve outcomes. It is an assessment of *"Can we do this?"*

Organizational Engagement focuses on "We" not "Me."

While acknowledging that the individual is important, organizational-level engagement focuses at the enterprise level! OE does not dismiss the value of the individual but acknowledges the critical nature of *organizational-level* performance. It focuses on how people work together across an organization to accomplish outcomes. All organizations have silos—groups of people who do not work together—for example: HR may not be working well with legal, accounts payable may not be working well with accounts receivable, operations is often siloed with sales. Assessments of organizational-level engagement reveal those silos. Once silos are identified, managers and leaders can improve how groups work together, share data, and make decision-making processes more effective.

The Six Elements of Organizational Engagement are *not* soft skills.

Organizational Engagement is comprised of six elements of organizational behavior. The bedrock for deriving these elements is the theory of Organizational Efficacy, first elaborated by my research in 2010.[55] The six elements of Organizational Engagement must be used to effect organizational change. They are anything but soft skills. Each of the six elements of OE represent hard work, focus, and long-range, determined effort.

How were the six elements of Organizational Engagement derived?

About two decades ago, I wanted to gain some exploratory insight based on my intuitions about Organizational Level Engagement. So, I conducted a study of 22 company executives asking the following question: "**In your professional opinion, which of these is most critical for building organizational strength and capabilities?" (Participants picked three and prioritized them.) Chart 3 shows their responses.**

Chart 3.

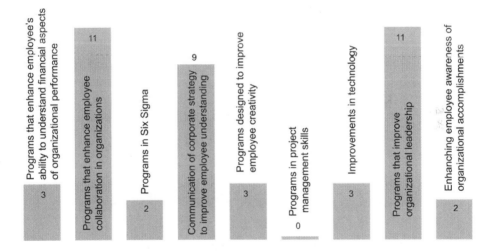

Which of these is most critical for building organizational strength and capabilities?

55   Bohn, J. G. (2010). "Development and Exploratory Validation of an Organizational Efficacy Scale." *HUMAN RESOURCE DEVELOPMENT QUARTERLY*, vol. 21, no. 3, Fall 2010, Wiley Periodicals, Inc. Published online in Wiley Online Library (wileyonlinelibrary. com) • DOI: 10.1002/hrdq.20048

Most interesting about this simple study of organizational leaders in multiple companies is the predominance of three key elements to build organizational success: (1) enhance employee collaboration, (2) improve communication, and (3) improve organizational leadership. Several of these elements were also identified by the noted social science researcher Albert Bandura. He wrote:

> "Belief of collective efficacy affects the sense of **mission** and purpose of a system, the strength of common **commitment** to what it seeks to achieve, how well its members **work together** to produce results, and the group's **resilience** in the face of difficulties."[56]

Having completed this study, I felt I was onto something and moved forward with my research. I worked with 22 organizations to statistically validate three elements of the scale. Modifying Bandura's language slightly, I designated three primary elements of Organizational Engagement:

1. **Clarity of Mission:** Do we know where we're going?

2. **Cohesion:** Can we work together?

3. **Commitment and Resilience:** Can we stay the course when things get tough? (Recall Bandura mentioned commitment).

Each of these elements was statistically validated by my research.[57]

I added two additional elements of organizational behavior because of their consistent appearance in the organizational literature: **Leadership**[58] and **Communication**

1. **Leadership Commitment:** How effective are leaders at getting things done?

2. **Communication:** How effective is the communication process in this organization?

Finally, a critical, yet rarely studied element of behavior was included to assess organizational engagement.

3. **Consequences / Accountability:** Are fair and just practices used to ensure that people are treated according to their work?

Consider this statement about accountability:

---

56   Bandura 1997, p. 469.
57   Bohn, J. G. (2010). *Ibid.*
58   The five Leadership questions in the BOES survey were statistically tested and validated in a separate unpublished study.

"Employees are aware of just about every wasted cost occurring throughout the enterprise. And to make sure they don't say too much or rock the boat too much, there's the culture, politics, and siloed management who see that only the changes they are comfortable will be made ."[59]

As you can see, these elements are dramatically different from Employee Engagement surveys, and they cover the critical, macro-level elements of organizational behavior.

Comparison: Employee Engagement versus Organizational-Level Engagement

The step beyond Employee Engagement is Organizational-Level Engagement. Note the differences:

Chart 4. Comparison of employee engagement and organizational engagement

Employee Engagement Focus	Organization Engagement Focus
... exclusively on what employees derive from the organization	...what the organization derives from all employees *working together*
... individual motivation—what's in it for *me*?	...organizational-level motivation—what's in it for *us*?
... local—personal—issues such as environment, pay, and benefits	*...organizational-level outputs* such as customer satisfaction, data quality, and leader effectiveness across groups.
... the leader the individual works with each day	...how all leaders work together across the enterprise each day and throughout the year
... "Me"	... "We"

---

59   Jim Smith, personal communication

The clear difference is the focus: Employee engagement focuses exclusively on what people want for themselves, whereas OE focuses on employee perceptions of organizational capabilities.

Characteristics of Organizations High in OE

Organizations that work hard on the six elements of OE have significant advantages in the marketplace. An organization high in OE displays many of the following characteristics:

▶ a high degree of morale

▶ employees want to be at work and to do the work

▶ enthusiastic workers who want to be part of an organization

▶ workers willing to take on a challenge

▶ workers who believe they are stronger than their competition

▶ a track record of accomplishments

▶ a team with a substantial vision for the future; persistence and evidence of innovation

These characteristics have value for recruitment and retention because people like winners![60]

The financial impact of each of these elements is clear.

Leaders who are conscious of organizational financials will see the logical fit between the elements of OE and financial outcomes. For example, Clarity of Mission focuses team members' energy toward specific tasks and goals, eliminating other choices. Cohesion increases efficiency and reduces unnecessary stress. Communication reduces anxiety and increases performance. Consequences reinforce the need for good work and cuts out bad actors. *Again, let me remind you that these are not "soft skills"—they have a direct bearing on organizational performance!*

---

60   Schneider, et al. (2003)

Even a cursory review of Chart 5 makes clear that each element of OE has a dramatic impact on organizational financial performance. Consider, for example, the influence of Cohesion on meeting budgets. If people don't work well together, decisions are delayed, data is hoarded, schedules are blocked, and on and on. Each of those behaviors makes or costs money!

Chart 5. Financial Outcomes and Organizational Engagement [61]

Factors that drive financial results	Clarity of Mission	Cohesion	Conviction / Resilience	Leadership Commitment	Communication	Consequences
ROI Budgets met	X	X	X	X	X	X
Opportunity Costs	X			X		
Productivity / Turnover		X		X	X	X
Process costs / waste / Inefficiency / Cycle time	X	X	X	X	X	X
Growth and Revenues	X	X		X		
Innovation		X				X
Leverage and Scale (2+2=5)	X			X		X

Organizational Engagement is necessary for financial success.

Organizational Engagement focuses on the organization's success, not just an individual or department. In a business world where competition accelerates, Organizational-Level Engagement is critical to success. One or two shining-star employees may be great to have in your organization, but to succeed, the organization must know how it operates at the enterprise level and how it shares information to make effective decisions that sustain success among all employees.

---

61   Graphic courtesy Lisa Howard

Transfer Industries:
"I think we're onto something that will change our organization."

Jennifer and Dale invited ten different high-potential leaders from across the organization to talk about what motivates employees.

Jennifer announced, "So, you're here to tell me the things that get people motivated, not just their personal sense of engagement, but the real energy they want to expend on their careers *in the context of this company*. Why this company? What makes them want to spend their time here? What gets them fired up and motivated?"

Participants looked at each other for a few seconds and hesitated.

Donald Amchez, Manager of Production, asked reluctantly: "Do you *really* want our insights?"

"Yes, absolutely," answered Jennifer. "We know we need to do something different. We want to do what's going to work for the company. Employee Engagement just isn't producing the results we expected."

Sheryl Kimble, Director of Engineering answered, "Well, people want to know what's happening. They want clear communication. That helps them understand what's going on. That energizes people for sure, and shuts down the rumor mill."

Ron Su, VP of Marketing, followed Sheryl. "They want to know the leadership here has a plan to get things done—that's a big one for me. Do leaders get things done? It gives them a sense that we know where we're going."

"And they tell me they admire the mission of the company—they like where it is going," said Phil Dalessio, Logistics Leader. He added, "And they like it when people work together, when leaders break down silos between departments."

"I think one big thing you're missing is accountability," Pravad Singh, CIO piped in. "People want to know others are held accountable for good work, and sometimes we need to get rid of bad actors who drag down the whole team. We don't do that very well around here, and it has a serious impact on our performance."

The room got quiet. *Everyone knew they were onto something.*

Because they were.

SECTION II— ANALYSIS

Chapter 6

The Six Elements of Organizational Engagement: Your Transformation Playbook

► This chapter presents a transformation playbook based in Organizational Engagement.

► The six elements of organizational engagement are: (1) Clarity of Mission, (2) Cohesion, (3) Communication, (4) Conviction (Resilience), (5) Leadership Commitment, and (6) Consequences (Accountability).

► This chapter provides a detailed analysis and explanation of each element.

The Heart of Organizational Engagement: The Six Elements

In the six chapters that follow, each of the elements of Organizational Engagement is reviewed from both an academic and practical perspective. The information presented is based on experience with hundreds of leaders in scores of organizations, including many among the Fortune 500. Each chapter provides insights from those who have led organizations teams and divisions, produced an ROI, and kept an organization financially solvent.

In this chapter, each element of Organizational Engagement is analyzed several ways.

A. **Reflection Questions** in the boxes at the beginning of the section should be deeply considered before moving into the text. Write down your answers, and think about them before reading further.

1. Some quantitative data is brought to bear on the subject.

2. Some academic research is provided.

3. Each chapter includes a practical development of the element.

   a. What is it?

   b. What does it do?

   c. How is it observed in the real world?

   d. Why won't employee engagement address these elements?

Take the time to read carefully through these chapters. Think through each element in depth in the context of *your organization.* Moving too quickly through this section is a mistake—it is worth taking the time to slow down. *Here's why:* So often, when we think about leadership, for example, we think we know what it is, so we simply charge on, perhaps because we've read other leadership books or because we've led groups. I encourage you to think deeply about each of these elements and the influence they have on your organization, your teams, and your people.

B. Look at this as a playbook, but *not a cookbook.*

Each of these elements is so important in organizations that they require more thinking than simply "do this and everything will be solved" (as if it were a cookbook for organizational success). These elements of organizational behavior impact your enterprise, so you will do well to think about each *in the context of your company or group. This exercise is not simply introducing "best practices" to add to your current system—it is an opportunity for you to think analytically about what is making your organization tick.*

C. Executives seeking a transformation playbook—here it is:

Directly analyzing your organization through the lens of each of these elements is an excellent starting point for transforming your company. Data-driven analysis requires the **B**ohn **O**rganizatlonal **E**ngagement **S**cale[62].

D. Read each section as a leadership team.

Consider reading through this section with your executive team to assess how things are going. You may be surprised by the differences in viewpoint—*and that may be part of the problem in your organization.*

Most importantly, the six elements of Organizational Engagement are NOT soft skills!

When leaders come to understand that the six elements of OE are not soft skills but behaviors requiring hard work, focus, and effort, they are on their way to transforming their organizations.

---

62   The 30-item Bohn Organizational Engagement Scale harvests data to assess the levels of the six elements of Organizational Engagement.

The Six Elements of Organizational Engagement as analyzed by the 30-Question Bohn Organizational Engagement Scale

1. **CLARITY of Mission.** Do we have confidence in where the organization is going?

2. **COHESION.** Can we work together to achieve mission outcomes?

3. **COMMUNICATION Effectiveness**. How well does the organization distribute critical information?

4. **CONVICTION.** Can we stay the course when times get tough?

5. **Leadership COMMITMENT.** Are our leaders capable of effectively achieving mission outcomes?

6. **CONSEQUENCES** Are people rewarded and recognized fairly?

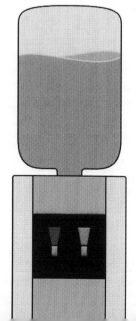

Chapter 7

Element #1: Clarity of Mission

"Do we have confidence in where we're going?"

REFLECTION QUESTIONS:

When people stand at the water cooler in your organization, how confident are they in the mission of your company? Could they say, without a doubt, that they know the direction of the company? Or would they say, "I'm not really sure what we're about. I'm not sure where we're going."

This first element of organizational engagement activates motivation by assuring individuals that their organization has a focused, thoughtful direction and that their leadership has a clear path to success. **Employees want to know they are not wasting time when they come to work.** *They want to know they work for an organization that has a future.*

"'Would you tell me, please, which way I ought to go from here?'
'That depends a good deal on where you want to get to,' said the Cat.
'I don't much care where —,' said Alice.
'Then it doesn't matter which way you go,' said the Cat."

—Lewis Carroll, *Alice in Wonderland*

The Mission Is Mission-Critical

"Failing to provide a clear superordinate goal, a clear mission or a vision, or failing to create clear order and purpose [for] the organization may result in employees struggling to become engaged; their need to understand what makes their work meaningful will be inhibited by their lack of a clear purpose."[63]

The research about why companies establish missions, goals, or objectives is exhaustive. Labovitz and Rosansky wrote an entire book devoted to the concept of organizational alignment, that is, the dedication

---

63   Byrne, 93.

of an organization to a common mission and purpose.[64] From a common-sense perspective, the purpose of a mission is to focus everyone in the same direction, whether there are 10 ten thousand employees. A mission reduces task uncertainty; people are more certain of *why* they are doing something. Lack of mission degrades the performance of the group.[65] If we don't know where we're going, we won't go anywhere, or we'll go everywhere. We also know that people spend an extraordinary amount of effort trying to understand their roles if mission clarity is lacking. Psychologists call it "communication overhead.[66]

Mission clarity is critical for organizational performance. The term *alignment* describes the phenomenon of "getting people on the same page." Yet organizational leadership rarely considers whether their mission (espoused theory) matches employee understanding (theory-in-practice)

Here's a hardball question: *Do your people really know where your organization is going? A tougher question for executives: Do you care about the mission of your organization or do you merely give it lip service?*

A little data to guide us

Once again, to validate my instincts, I conducted a random survey with over 200 respondents asking: ***"What are the greatest challenges facing your organization today?"***[67] Here are the results:

200+ global respondents

"What are the greatest challenges facing your organization today?"

Scale: 10 = Deeply Concerned
1 = Not at All Concerned

Teams not working together to accomplish goals	6.72
Uncertainty about organizational direction	6.69

---

64 1997 Organizational Dynamics Inc.
65 Howell & Dipboye, 1982, p. 98.
66 MacMillan, J., Elliot, E., & Serfaty, D. "Communication Overhead: The hidden cost of team cognition" in *Team Cognition, Salas & Fiore* (2009), Washington D. C.: APA press.
67 Participants were offered a free white paper if they answered ten questions.

Too many disconnected initiatives	6.61
Other leaders are ineffective when communicating	6.56
Too much change going on at the same time	6.28
Employee uncertainty slows productivity	6.10
Frustrated employees want to give up	6.03
Initiatives with no possibility of success	5.88
People not pulling their weight	5.66
You are ineffective in your communication style	5.52[68]

The number-one issue across the board was "Teams not working together to accomplish goals" followed by "Uncertainty about organizational direction." After conducting some simple correlations with the data, I learned this: There was a .79 correlation between these two phenomena: "Uncertainty about organizational direction" and "Uncertainty slows productivity."[69] In other words, clarity of mission is essential for having all leaders and team members moving in the same direction. The data confirmed my intuition.

> ### What's the impact of organizational uncertainty? Missing a mission.

---

68   Note the one-point difference in perceptions of communication, self vs. others!
69   Cohen's (1992) generally accepted conventions to interpret effect size (small = >.10; medium = >.30; large = >.50) for Pearson correlation coefficients. Cohen, J. (1992). A power primer. *Psychological Bulletin, 112*, 155-159.

If people in an organization are unsure of where they are headed, they will be uncertain about what they should do, which undermines collective engagement, the ability to work together toward a common goal. Lack of clear direction causes the following:

- Employee anxiety

- Employee uncertainty

- Inhibits risk-taking

- Slows innovation

- Wait-and-see attitudes (a.k.a "hostile compliance")

- Social loafing (sitting on the sidelines until someone provides direction)

Thus, a sense of mission or purpose is a critical factor in organizational engagement. In a study of corporate culture, Denison wrote,

"A mission provides purpose and meaning, as well as a host of non-economic reasons why the work of the organization is important. Second, a sense of mission provides clear direction and goals that serve to define the appropriate course of action for the organization and its members."[70]

Further, "in successful corporations…, a shared sense of the broad term goals of the firm helps to structure behavior…. A sense of mission requires that organizations apply *future perfect thinking.*[71]" In other words, a mission helps people focus their energies on things that guide them to accomplish a desired future.

This is consistent with the research conducted by Kotter and Heskett (1992), which states that the "cultural strength" of a company is a result of goal alignment. In a firm with a strong culture, employees tend to "march to the same drummer."[72] The idea of *knowing which way we're going* is essential to organizational engagement. It is the first element in OE for a reason. Whatever work is to be done in an organization must be centered around a future vision and mission. We do not want to waste precious employee time or motivation, and we do not want to waste corporate resources. People need to know they are accomplishing something to feel successful, because success motivates!

---

70   Denison, 13
71   Ibid., 14
72   p. 16

Mission is the guide for everything

In his seminal book on organizational learning, Senge (1990) wrote, "If any one idea about leadership has inspired organizations for thousands of years, it's the capacity to hold a shared picture of the future we seek."[73] Mission is a shared mental concept of a possible future that members of an organization can attain *together*; it is a shared cognition of what can be. So critical is the concept that Senge devotes an entire chapter in his book on organizational learning to what he calls "shared vision."[74]

In their research, Larson and LaFasto (1989) wrote:

"It is rare to discover anything in the realm of human behavior that occurs with great consistency… Therefore, it was surprising to find that in every case, without exception, when an effectively functioning team was identified, it was described by the respondent as having *a clear understanding of its objective* (italics mine)."[75]

They sum it up by saying, "The more an individual or a group of people have a clear understanding of the nature of the problem that confronts them, the more effective they will be at solving that problem."[76] Harvard cognitive psychologist Robert Sternberg said long ago that clarity in what we want to accomplish helps us rule out other avenues of thought, focusing our cognitive energy to get things done.[77] Mission is critical!

A question on the famous Q12 employee engagement survey confirms the importance of mission [78] "The mission/purpose of my company makes me feel my job is important." A mission is what social scientists call a "superordinate goal"—something bigger than all the individual employees in an organization.

All this academic research points to a fundamental truth: **A sense of mission is the first element of organizational engagement**. An organization uncertain about its mission and future is unlikely to be high in

73 p. 9.
74 He identifies several outcomes of a shared vision: "When people truly share a vision they are connected, bound together by a common aspiration . . . A shared vision, especially one that is intrinsic, uplifts people's aspirations" (p. 206). "Visions are exhilarating" (p. 207). "In a corporation, a shared vision changes people's relationship with the company… A shared vision is the first step in allowing people who mistrusted each other to begin to work together." In fact, an organization's sense of purpose, vision, and operating values establish the most basic level of commonality" (p. 208). "Shared visions compel courage…" (p. 208). "Shared vision fosters risk taking and experimentation" (p. 209).
75 p. 27
76 p. 28
77 Sternberg, 1997
78 Harter, Schmidt and Hayes.

organizational engagement. And though organizations provide annual kick-off meetings to tell their employees about the mission, the bigger question is: how far into the organization does the mission resonate? In short, do people understand it and is their daily work guided by it?

The **B**ohn **O**rganizational **E**ngagement **S**cale [BOES] includes four questions that focus on Clarity of MISSION.

Employee Engagement and Employee Experience do not address the Element of Mission — here's why:

Employee engagement is focused exclusively on the individual experience of the employee, and while the mission of the organization may be something employees hear about, EE does not assess mission in the context of the organization.

The Employee Experience is a direct *result* of the mission, for without clear direction, people will be uncertain, anxious and unsure about their role in the company.

Now that you've had an opportunity to read through and think about the element of mission and purpose, how would you rate your organization?

*We have **not** focused on Mission*   *We are effectively managing Mission*

1   2   3   4   5   6   7   8   9   10

Elements of organizational engagement analysis

1. Do we know where we're going?

Chapter 8
Element #2: Workforce Cohesion
"Can we work together?"

REFLECTION QUESTIONS:

When people stand at the water cooler in your organization, do they have a sense that people are truly collaborative and can work together to get things done? Do people feel they like and respect each other? Do people sense organizational silos that keep groups separate?

This second element of organizational engagement activates motivation by assuring individuals that their effort is part of something bigger that is effectively coordinated to bring about organizational achievements.

Teamwork is a common thread on LinkedIn and other business social media; often the word *collaboration* is used as a synonym. Clearly the notion of people working together is nothing new, but in the context of OE, people working together increases productivity and eases organizational tensions. In OE, we call it the element of Cohesion.

Cohesion is the power activated when leaders and people in an organization effectively coordinate and marshal resources and collaborate on activities to accomplish organizational ends. Cohesion is much bigger than *collaboration*. Cohesion is the ability of an entire organization to work together, a critical factor in organizational engagement. Howell and Dipboye (1982), in their study of industrial psychology, state: "High levels of individual effort may not ensure that the group will be effective in its performance of its tasks, since, on many tasks, members must coordinate their efforts with other members."[79] A group's ability to coordinate efforts is

---

79   p. 94. Conversely, (b) "Intergroup conflict lessens the performance of the whole organization" (p. 103); (c) "Performance usually depends on the degree to which members coordinate their efforts" (p. 98) and the level of coordination; (d) They go on to say that one of the keys to group process is the ability to coordinate efforts (p. 119). And finally, (e)

critical to success, and groups who compete within organizations cause inefficiencies (also known as silos). Coordination of action is powerful stuff. Coordination of action is cohesion. Cohesion is NOT a soft skill. It takes effortful leadership and mission focus.

Can we work together?

The culture that leaders build either increases or decreases cohesion, through example, coaching, and follow-up. Kotter and Heskett (1992) state that in an organization where leaders have developed a strong culture, "Members actively support one another's efforts to identify all problems and implement workable solutions."[80]

Supportive and collaborative relationships with coworkers increase performance in high-stress jobs (Robbins, 1998). In short, people helping people makes organizational life a bit easier. Researchers have demonstrated that cohesion is *negatively correlated to task conflict.* [81] In other words, people that worked together effectively had *lower task conflict.* Clearly, working together has significant organizational benefits. In fact, for the organization to see true transformational change, cohesion is mandatory.

In their famous work on industrial psychology, Katz and Kahn (1978) state it this way:

> "Three categories of behavior are required to achieve high levels of organizational effectiveness. People must join and remain in the organization; they must perform dependably the roles assigned to them; and *they must engage in occasional innovative and cooperative behavior beyond the requirements of the role but in service of organizational objectives.*"[82]

If people go beyond their normal work roles to support others, the organization will see the benefits. Team members who are effective and competent aid the success of the organization, and other team members know if they have team members who are "the real deal." Teams that work together well add power to the entire group, increasing organizational engagement. Thus, **cohesion** is that ability of a large group of people to work together to achieve ends, both at the team, division, and organizational level. Cohesion is the second major element of organizational engagement.

"Groups in organizations often experience stress in the form of competition or conflict with other groups" (p. 102). This tells us that coordination of actions is crucial to organizational success.

80   p. 44
81   Gelfland, Leslie, Keller and de Drue (2012)
82   p. 424, italics mine

We're supposed to work together, but we don't—hindrances to cohesion.

Cohesion is essential to organizational success. I state the obvious. In an organization without cohesion, people make decisions without including significant stakeholders which leads to incomplete decisions and ineffective implementation. The culture that leaders build either increases or decreases collaboration, through example, through coaching and through follow-up.

Here are some common barriers to cohesion:

1. **Overload**: Inattention to the number of current projects prevents team members from working together. People simply don't have enough time to get to everything.

2. **My pet project**: Excess attention to a few projects causes some team members to work exclusively on things they like.

3. **Politics**: "Who is getting rewarded for what?" has a heavy influence on cohesion.

4. **Failure to challenge the non-participants:** When we allow social loafers on a team, we can expect a lack of cohesion.

5. **Departmental turf:** Some groups insulate themselves from the rest of the organization to ensure a place of prominence.

6. **No common ground:** When the overall goal is not understood, people find it difficult to participate.

7. **Too much effort:** The energy required to understand the intricacies of the related action overwhelms the participants.

8. A more philosophical underpinning of a fear of collaboration is the notion of the dreaded **committee**. If we collaborate, people will be forced to work with others they don't like.

9. Belief that collaboration **decelerates decision-making**.

10. Belief that collaboration **hinders action**.

11. The altruistic belief that people will naturally work together is Pollyannaish. It's about **leaders building environments** that create collaborative teams.

12. Managers believe that the mere act of delegation will automatically generate teams that work together, but delegation alone isn't enough. Managers who demand cohesion are setting themselves up for failure. But managers who model it remove all the excuses of their underlings. Cohesion does not happen automatically.

Considering cohesion in-depth

Throughout our working lives, we have joined forces with people, either willingly, (as in a volunteer organization) or unwillingly (as in being put on the same team in a work environment with someone we don't want to work with). In the end, however, the goal of our time together was to advance some cause or complete a task or project.

People should work together, shouldn't they? So why don't they?

Cohesion is a good thing. We all know that...at least in principle. So, the question is, why *don't* people work together like they should? Gaining an insight into this phenomenon is crucial for organizations interested in increasing OE, since often the only way to improve implementation speed and synergy of ideas is to work together.

Consultants face this dilemma every time they work with a client attempting organizational change. The literature is filled with the need for collaboration, but the issue of why people can seem to "get along" seems conspicuously absent, like the elephant in the room.

Perhaps it's because we're all a little guilty of not working together like we should, or maybe it's because we don't like the negativity, but let's face it: cohesion is a powerful element of OE. The speed at which an organization executes strategies and the effectiveness of change happening in organizations is a factor of mission, focus, and cohesion. We are co-laborers, meaning we work *together* to get the job done.

A little research to ground the theory

As you know by now, my approach is to find practical, ground-level data to support theory. So, I posed a question to scores of people, including consulting, management and HR professionals across a wide global population to assess *why people can't seem to work together*. The responses are clustered around several different themes, along with some suggestions about how we might go about managing these issues to collaborate better. The purpose for this section is to provide you with insight from peers across the world. It is intended to build your awareness of the challenges to cohesion.

Participants were asked to complete the following open-ended sentence:

"People in organizations have a difficult time working together because…"

One person responded with a fine synopsis of the issue.

"One could write a book or two on the subject. We, not "people", have a difficult time working with one another for a variety of reasons that are complex (involving many factors), dynamic (the factors interact in ever-changing ways), and often mysterious (unpredictable, uncontrollable, and unavoidable)."

—Organizational Consultant

Six themes emerged. According to those surveyed, people in organizations have a difficult time working together for the following reasons:

> (1) I'm only human!
>
> (2) Personality Differences and Conflicts
>
> (3) Personal…and Hidden Agendas
>
> (4) Perceived Fairness and Lack of Trust
>
> (5) Individualistic Management Practices
>
> (6) Inability to Deal with Conflict

I'll take each of these categories in turn and offer some suggestions for consideration as we deal with this important element of cohesion. Without an answer to this question, leaders and managers will find it difficult to get groups to work together. Simply knowing that these realities exist, as opposed to having a rose-colored view of how people "should" work together, will go a long way in assisting teams.

1. I'm only human!

The first reason for our inability to work together appears to be deeply fundamental, almost as if it is in our DNA. Several respondents suggested that fear and selfishness are reasons people may not work together. For example:

People in organizations have a difficult time working together because...

"People in organizations have a difficult time working together because they feel threatened by today's highly competitive work environment in which skills and competencies change as technology changes."

—*Innovation and learning consultant*

"People in organizations have a difficult time working together because they are human... and that's what happens with humans every now and again, particularly in an environment where they don't choose those they are with or they spend too long with them that even the little things get annoying."

—Consultant

"Selfishness: I want my agenda and do all I can to make it happen. If you and I can negotiate a 'win-win' deal, fine. But if we can't, it becomes difficult to work with one another. There are numerous factors relating to selfishness. It is simply a fact of life.

—President of a Consulting Firm

Opportunities for improvement

It is unlikely that we can change the fundamentals of human nature. Research publications attest to the reality that people fear new things and new people, and fear and discomfort take them people of their comfort zone, thus making it difficult to work together, at least initially. As to selfishness, that is a characteristic that might be better stated as "what's in it for me?" Anyone who has worked with groups understands that American culture pushes individualism in the way of of individual accomplishments and thus fosters a refined (and self-justifying) sense of selfishness.

2. Personality Differences and Conflicts

A second major reason people have a tough time working together is because they have underlying personality differences. This is not hard to understand. We all grow up in different environments; we react differently to different foods, music, and events. Every person has a unique life history that may match some of the vectors and tangents of the lives of others, but most of the time, we see the universe through our eyes. And anyone who has studied the Big Five personality inventory[83] knows how difficult it is to change personality. It should not surprise us that our individual differences should be a major factor in our inability to work together.

People in organizations have a difficult time working together because...

"because many people have a very difficult time separating the personal from the professional..."

—Dean of a College

"People in organizations find it difficult to work together because of the wide variety of personalities, characteristics, and opinions each member of the organization may have. Trying to put these things aside and focus on the one common point that brings the group together is sometimes difficult to do.

—Administrator

"Some are introverts, shy, have limited cognitive or emotional intelligence, dogmatic, know-it-alls, lazy, have significant factual belief, attitude, or value differences, politics, ambition, unwillingness to take risks, devalue opinions and thoughts of others, are lousy communicators, poor listening skills... the list could go on forever."

—Professor

---

83   John, O. P., & Srivastava, S. (1999). The Big-Five trait taxonomy: History, measurement, and theoretical perspectives. In L. A. Pervin & O. P. John (Eds.), *Handbook of personality: Theory and research* (Vol. 2, pp. 102–138). New York: Guilford Press.

"because ...

they are driven by different goals/objectives that may clash

they lack emotional maturity

they lack the interpersonal skills necessary for resolving complex interpersonal situations."

—Sales executive and trainer

"More often than not between two or more people of similar personality. Two extraverted aggressive types butt heads, etc."

—President of a Consulting Firm

"Because of personality differences. Personalities which complement each other are rarely considered when work groups are chosen."

—Consultant and college professor

Opportunities for improvement

So, how do we deal with this? Let's start by getting this issue out in the open instead of hiding it. Expecting everyone to match leader's behavior or expectations simply doesn't make sense. It's advantageous to discuss personality differences and how that can help the group process. It relieves some pressure to conform by acknowledging that people are simply going to be different. Getting comfortable with the differences—that makes the difference!

Sometimes I think the greatest diversity issue we experience is not gender or race, but the broad varieties of experiences we have all had in our lives, and how they have shaped us[84]. Let's face it: we are all products of years of decisions, learning, travel, and interactions, and we have formulated our view of the world through our experience. Acknowledging and respecting this reality is a good starting point in understanding how to build cohesion.

---

84   Also known as "cognitive diversity"

3. Personal... and hidden... agendas

Here we find some of the most unpleasant stuff about why collaboration doesn't take place. Personal agendas are always lurking the background for every employee. Don't like the sound of that? It's true. "Aye! There's the rub." Recent books on power, like Kathleen Reardon's Secret Handshake: Mastering the politics of the business inner circle, share insights into this side of human nature.[85]

People in organizations have a difficult time working together because...

"Hidden agendas."

—Senior Analyst, Education & Organization Development

"People in organizations have a difficult time working together because... they have different needs and goals. In short, what motivates each person to behave as they do may be totally different, which can lead to conflict.

—Professor, New Zealand

"Ideological conflicts: What I generally refer to as conflicting perspectives related to beliefs, values, and desires. This discussion generally takes the form of what we think we 'ought' to do."

—President of a Consulting Firm.

"We are able to see the faults and inconsistencies of others, but not our own. We are better at understanding the motives of others than we are our own. It all makes for a big mess. By the grace of God, we are able to get something done sometimes anyway.

—Pastor

---

85   Reardon, K. (2002) *The Secret Handshake: Mastering the Politics of the Business Inner Circle Currency*: New York

"People come to the table with different agendas. People are held accountable for the completion of their part of the project not the whole."

—Training Project Manager

"Turf battles, power struggles."

—Senior Analyst, Education & Organization Development

Opportunities for improvement

An "agenda" is really about need fulfillment, power, gains, a desire to accomplish something from one's efforts, recognition, feeling valued, being "heard," and about showing the world personal competence. Managers must recognize this as they assemble teams. It's the elephant in the room that must be acknowledged. People have goals in mind whether they undertake a new job or a new assignment. Personal fulfillment is naturally expected as a goal in the grand scheme of what makes people tick. People work so they can gain promotions, and the income commensurate with greater responsibility and a better position.

Personal agendas will always exist, but great leadership carefully constructs how personal agendas will accomplish something greater, and showing (really demonstrating) how putting aside their individual agendas for a greater good is better over the long haul for everyone's benefit. That means leaders must know their people well!

With regard to turf wars and power battles, the only people who can really solve (or exacerbate) that issue are leaders at the very top of the organization through their example. Their example will be pervasive in its effects, either for good or ill. People watch how top leaders sort things out. Thus, it's the greater agenda, for the greater good and the organization's mission, that must be the overall focus.

4. Perceived Fairness and Lack of Trust

Another key issue that arose in the research is the idea of perceived fairness. In other words, is everyone doing his or her part? Is social loafing happening within my work circle, and am I picking up the slack? Is everyone pulling their weight? What happens at the end of a project? Will people remember the long hours I put in and the time I sacrificed? The family relationships that were strained because of my time away? Am I being heard? All of these needs point to one thing: people want to be treated equitably.

People in organizations have a difficult time working together because...

"People in organizations have a difficult time working together because... they perceive themselves as working harder than their coworkers, that their contribution is more important than their coworkers', which leads to resentment."

—Web Developer

"People in organizations have a difficult time working together because people have different work ethics."

—Accountant

"People in organizations find it difficult to work together because... they don't know their co-workers and are very suspicious of their co-workers' intentions. New people... will find it difficult since there is a natural barricade that seems to go up until the new person 'proves' their worth to the group. Sometimes, there may also be the fear of infringement into one's territory—afraid that someone else will either take credit for or undermine the others' work."

—Administrator

"Issues of trust; more often than not caused by incongruent behavior. I say I will do something, but don't. When my espoused theory (it is important to provide timely feedback) is significantly different than my theory-in-use (I seldom actually give such feedback), people begin to view me as dishonest and lacking integrity. Trust begins to break down so that people have a difficult time working together.

—President of a Consulting Firm

"Lack of appreciation for the inclusion of all ideas and Organizational Politics"

—Senior Analyst, Education & Organization Development

Opportunities for improvement

Managers and consultants can build trust among teams. Being careful of how leaders criticize people on the team is a major issue, since one person may see criticism as unfair and others may in turn take advantage of the situation. People have a sharp and keen sense of fairness which is rooted in their experiences as children.[86]

The recognition process used in teams is crucial in avoiding perceived unfairness, whether it is the amount of time the manager spends with individuals or how much time they spend together outside the workplace. Fairness issues must be dealt with quickly. Delaying the resolution of such issues only breeds a greater misperception of inequity and spurs on conversations that focus energy on fairness and not the task at hand.

5. Business climate of Individual accomplishments versus group accomplishments

One pervasive issue in the study revolved around individualistic management practices.

People in organizations have a difficult time working together because...

"Because of the competitive nature intrinsic to many business environments—competition for power, for advancement, for rewards, etc."

—Consultant and college professor

---

86   I'll discuss this more in the chapter on Accountability and Consequences.

"People in organizations have a difficult time working together because American organizations design so much of their work and rewards to emphasize individual accountability and accomplishments. These organizational designs reflect American culture's high valuing of individuality as opposed to group identity in all of its social institutions."

–Professor of Business

"People in organizations have a difficult time working together because... the recognition/reward system supports individual accomplishment and puts employees and team members at odds."

—Training Analyst and Consultant

".... because management often creates and sustains competitive rather than collaborative environments."

—Professor

"People in organizations have a difficult time working together because... everyone looks to individual gains at the cost of overall group/organizational interests, organizational politics plays a larger part in rewards than fair evaluations."

—Assistant professor faculty of management studies

University of Delhi India

"Emphasis on individual contributions versus teamwork"

—Senior Analyst - Education & Organization Development

Opportunities for improvement

We need to face the reality that people have personal dreams and goals, which are supported by their work. People will not work for nothing. Even altruism brings people fulfillment. Having said that, American individualism influences how people feel about accomplishments. It is so wired into our culture that the normal way to influence cohesion is through shared rewards and bonuses, based on the performance of the group.

6. Inability to resolve and confront difficult issues

Although it was only mentioned once, conflict is an issue looming in the background of the collaborative process. It takes skill and savvy, along with good role models, to sort out conflict. People simply don't like conflict. It is unpredictable, and sometimes flat out scary with uncertain outcomes. Careers are sometimes damaged or impacted in conflict situations.

People in organizations have a difficult time working together because…

"Most people, as sender or receiver, do not have the COURAGE or SKILLS to confront uncomfortable situations."

—Industrial Psychologist and Trainer

Opportunities for improvement

Dealing with conflict is a delicate matter. People's egos are at stake.. Since people do not know the outcomes of conflict, they are unwilling to engage it. Ultimately, this may be the one characteristic that separates the best managers and consultants from the mediocre, since the ability to manage conflict is crucial to ensuring people "get along."

In a non-profit organization that I was part of, I witnessed a wounded ego, and how it contributed to conflict and ultimately the resignation of a person from the team. No matter how delicately these things are handled, conflict is about ego, pride, and all life's deep, tough stuff. If all parties can walk away with dignity and self-respect at the end of a conflict, we can move forward. In addition, an element of forgetfulness along with a sense of humor is a tool to bring resolution to difficult human situations.

My personal perspective on why it is difficult to build cohesion: the "superstar"

I believe one of the reasons people find it difficult to work together is the varying level of focus and intensity of different team members. No matter who we work with, or under what circumstances, an interesting dynamic arises: someone knows the way to solve a problem, or is relatively sure they know the way. If they do not have the patience to wait for others to catch up, or they cannot articulate their point clearly enough, they will get frustrated waiting for the rest of the team.

In some instances, there are team members, who—because of having "been there, done that," training, or just flat-out brilliance—can see "the way things ought to be." (Quite often, they are right!) When they are part of a team, however, they will manifest a desire to move forward more quickly and perceive others as laggards, which causes resentment and irritation in the ranks. Team members will only come around if the person leading has a strong success rate in past projects.

Conclusion

People find it difficult to work together for many reasons. Just being aware of the things discussed above helps us to shift into a positive direction, acknowledging that getting people to work together will not be easy. Helping people see a mission greater than their own agenda is a step in the right direction. Providing people with consistent feedback and constancy of purpose will also help them overcome some of their obstacles to getting along.

But, let's face it, from the time we're very young, we start with a self to feed, clothe, and fulfill. Those deep needs are not going away. So, the secret is to use the personal agendas of all for the benefit of the whole team. This will takes managerial work and effort, but the successful companies of the future must make a diligent effort to solve this problem today.

An unexpected finding

What I found conspicuously absent in the responses I received was a mention of issues of diversity, gender, or racial inequality. While this is a small sample and it's not representative of all populations, it shows that the barriers of working together to achieve a common goal probably transcend diversity, gender, or race. In addition, the global experts who reviewed this book prior to press made little mention of diversity or gender. What they did say, however, was that many of these issues resonated in their personal experience in the workplace.

The Bohn Organizational Engagement Scale [BOES] includes eight questions that focus on COHESION

Employee Engagement and Employee Experience do not address element of Cohesion. Here's why:

Employee engagement is focused exclusively on the individual experience of the employee, EE does not ask questions that address cohesion—working together—in the context of the organization. EE does not ask how people are working together—or even if they are willing to work together.

The Employee Experience is a direct result of cohesion. If people cannot work together—or worse, won't work together—people will be frustrated and ineffective in their daily work. That's a big part of everyday experience.Now that you've had an opportunity to think about cohesion how would you rate your organization?

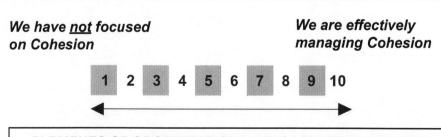

We have _not_ focused on Cohesion

We are effectively managing Cohesion

1 2 3 4 5 6 7 8 9 10

ELEMENTS OF ORGANIZATIONAL ENGAGEMENT ANALYSIS
1. Do we know where we're going?
2. Can we work together?

Chapter 9

Element #3: Communication
Do we know what's going on?

REFLECTION QUESTIONS:

When people stand at the water cooler in your organization, how confident would they be that they knew what was happening at the strategic and local level?

This third element of Organizational Engagement activates employee motivation by reassuring individuals that information is flowing effectively and that people have the information they need in order to make good decisions and move forward without wasting time. In organizations with high OE, people know what's going on.

Communication has a major impact on organizations.

"A Classic is something everyone wants to have read, but no one wants to read."

—Mark Twain

In over four decades of observing organizations teaching graduate business classes, and working as a manager, leader, and consultant, I have observed one chronic organizational issue. It is the one element of organizational behavior everyone talks about yet does little to improve. To paraphrase Twain: *Communications is the issue everyone wants solved, but no one wants to solve.* And yet, communication is an essential element of organizational engagement.

How organizational communication shows up in the real world

The chart below was gathered by students in one of my MBA classes at a major university. One of their assignments was to interview five members of their organizations on "*What brings the components of an organization together to achieve an outcome?*" (their interviews provided an unbiased data pool—no one could manipulate the output – whatever showed up showed up).

As you can see from the collected data, communication was the #1 behavior necessary for achieving organizational outcomes. I have conducted this exercise multiple times with different classes and students from across the world over the past decade. they always reach same conclusion: **Communication is a predominant factor in organizational behavior—it is the glue that ties everything together.**

Chart 6. How organizations manage behavior

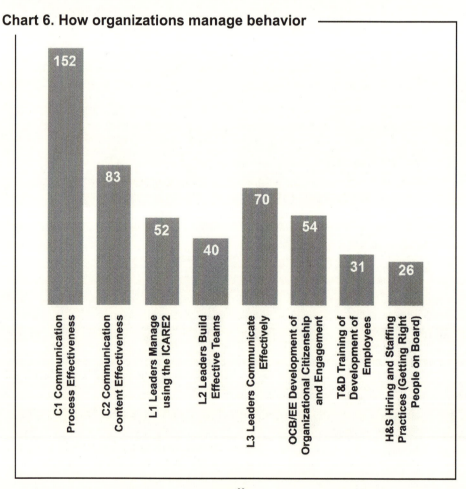

The results from another analysis of Organizational Behavior

Another class in Organizational Behavior included over thirty graduate students in the medical field, government, manufacturing, travel agencies, law, service industries, retail, and more, along with students from several parts of the world. In short, the output of their interviews was representative of just about every domain of employment.

The class was surprised by a few discoveries about ineffective communication: (1) few members of their organizations knew their company's Mission[87], (2) clarity was lacking in directions and decisions, and (3) follow-up was nonexistent. In other words, though communication is important, the students discovered it was weak.

The fact is people want to know: *What's goin' on?*

- The "need to know basis" is patronizing and counterproductive. Managers must remove this phrase from their communication habits. Organizational bias must be towards more communication, not less.

- When people feel left out or uninformed, they feel slighted. "Informational justice" is a term used to clarify that people believe they have been told the truth.[88] Keeping them informed is a way for them to feel treated justly and with respect.

Without effective organizational communication:

- People make mistakes, and those mistakes can be costly to a business and to other people!

- Ineffective communication stifles energy and leads to low productivity—because more time is spent on misunderstandings between people than on organizational output.

- Misunderstood goals can lead to redundancy and/or conflicting efforts.

- Misunderstood goals cause misdirection of effort, wasting time and money.

- Misunderstood definitions of terms like "Deployment" or "Change Management" can cause confusion.

---

87   John Kotter, Harvard Business School professor and change management expert, famously wrote, "Most companies under communicate their visions for change by at least a factor of 10." Kotter, J. (2011, June 14). "Think You're Communicating Enough? Think Again." *Forbes*. Retrieved from https://www.forbes.com/sites/johnkotter/2011/06/14/think-youre-communicating-enough-think-again/#3debd5236275

88   Foster, p. 11

- Misunderstood instructions—the details required to effectively use one's energy—cause people to waste time, which corrodes employee motivation.

- Cognitive psychology tells us that people will fill in the blanks when communication is missing. When people feel like they're left out, grapevine communication (rumors, incomplete data, assumptions) becomes the norm.

What are the key business benefits of effective communications?

1. Communication provides a context for decision-making, allowing people to sort things out among competing priorities, thus focusing their energies.

2. All communications provide a context for prioritization. What do I need to do to support the organization? What is the best use of my time?

3. Communication increases speed of decision-making by ensuring correct and accurate content has been shared.

4. Communication develops trust in leadership.

5. Communication prevents the grapevine from taking over.

6. Communication stops rumors dead in their tracks.

Myriad self-help books, sitcoms, and radio programs tell us couples don't communicate effectively. If two people who are close to one another in daily life do not find communication to be easy, what should we expect in the workplace that is loaded with political minefields and a demanding work schedule? People are pressed for time to communicate, but this is a *"pay me now or pay me later"* situation. Managers do not have the luxury of NOT communicating for the sake of expedience.

My definition of good communication

Simply put, good organizational communication is a clearly understood combination of direction and decision. My definition of communication? "Proactively turning intentions into reality." **Proactively** means not waiting to communicate. **Intentions** are those wild cognitive adventures going on inside our minds which mean nothing to anyone until we carefully reveal our thought process. **"Reality"** is the world we live in, the place where tangible output occurs—the place where we can see, hear, and touch our initial intentions. *In short, good communication brings order out of chaos!* It flows through two major vectors: **Direction** and **Decision**.

1. **Direction is the "Why?"** Providing direction is a powerful form of communication. because we can't do, as Yogi Berra said, "If you see a fork in the road, take it." Direction clears a path for hearers and followers. An organizational Mission is purpose. A team charter is purpose. Goal-setting is purpose. Each of these provides direction.

2. **Decisions are the "What?"** In the words of many stakeholders, "What are we doin'?" Decisions eliminate options that can cause confusion, ensuring people save time and precious human effort. Decisiveness is a hallmark of great leaders.

Before we go any further! Good content is key!

I'm going to lay out a bunch of details on the communication process. Lest there be any doubt: no amount of process effectiveness will overcome bad content. The content of communication—the symbols, details, precision, and organization of the material—are the essence of the messaging to your organization. Take the time to get the content right! *Bad content is worse than no content.*

Specific Communications Content

1. **Coordination of activities**: Getting people together takes effort, clear focus, clear agendas. Who is doing what and when?

2. **Knowledge of the future**: "People here expect leaders in this business to know where they're going." It includes things like Vision: What is the overall goal of a project or strategic initiative?

3. **Knowledge of roles and expectations:** Who has what responsibilities? Instruction: How do things work? Expectations: What kind of quality do we want?

4. **Knowledge of what has happened:** So people can feel a sense of achievement, movement, and momentum and so people can know if they're on track. Which decisions have been made? Do we need to make a course correction? What is now a lower priority and what do we stop doing?

5. **Knowledge of victories**: Allowing people to feel the emotional sense of achievement and build confidence for the next project. Who has gone above and beyond? Does the organization know how good it is?

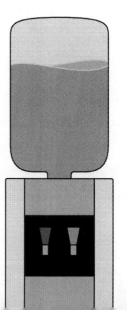

COMMUNICATION PROCESS:

To effectively communicate, a manager or leader simply must:

1. Gain the attention of the listener or hearer.

2. Confirm the attention of the listener or hearer.

3. Carefully articulate the issue, request, instruction, or goal.

4. Have the listener confirm what you said in their words.

5. Ask something like: "Are we on the same page?" and check for eye contact or other *evidence that the message got through*.

6. If, at that point, a person says they understand and agrees with you, they own the outcome going forward.[89]

7. Check-ins: Weekly huddles are an effective tool.

Barriers to Effective Communication

Effective communication rarely happens in today's organizations: *Here are some barriers.*

Barrier #1: Not enough communication.

Executives are vulnerable to the belief that their words and concepts will be carried out, largely because of their positional power. Executives simply believe that one-time communication is going to work because of their role in the organization. But that simply isn't true. Without follow-up, nothing is certain. *"Follow-up or foul up."*

---

89   The British Navy taught seamen to say, "Aye, aye, sir!" The first "aye" was to acknowledge that they had hear and understood. The second "aye" was an agreement that they would do what they were told.

Barrier #2: Leaders don't take the time to focus their communications.

Leaders don't take the time to develop thoughtful communication by considering their audience. I've met people in the field who did NOT have a computer and didn't know a thing about what was happening at corporate. We needed to get paper to them. Even in this day and age, they still needed paper instructions. That takes focus. Ineffective focus prevents connection. Communication takes effort.

A moment of focus is communication power! Focus is key to good communication. Focus takes leadership effort. *But is it true that managers don't have time?* Communication takes effort. **Solution:** Take the time to be clear. Often a thorough five-minute conversation can solve a world of future pain, but it requires deliberate focus.

Barrier #3: Perfection paralysis.

Managers fear communicating something that could change. Managers are afraid of communicating something incomplete. Therefore, they do *nothing,* and their people remain in the dark.

Barrier #4: Haste and sound bites.

Speed degrades effectiveness. Our organizations are moving so fast these days that managers frequently provide employees with sound bites of information. This includes perhaps twenty seconds of information shared in a hallway conversation between meetings, which develops into misunderstandings that occur when dialogue does not take place. People want (and often need) additional clarity, but they are not given the opportunity because managers don't have (or won't take) the time.

Barrier #5: The increased complexity and volume of Instant Messaging, texting, and other technology are forcing people into cognitive overload.

Research on multitasking demonstrates the ineffectiveness of doing too much at one time.

Barrier #6: The walls between us—silos degrade contact.

Silos keep things separate. Silos are great for farms, not for organizations! Organizations often do not coordinate activities because of silo mentalities within their organizations, so one message often runs counter to another. This is a management-communication issue that extends well beyond the rank-and-file personnel in the trenches.

Strangely enough, organizations still have silos! Twenty-five years ago, Geary Rummler found that the greatest opportunities for improvement in most organizations could be found in the white spaces between the silos in an organization chart. It is still true today.[90]

Barrier #7: Four ridiculous communication assumptions:

a. One of the worst barriers to communication is that managers assume that people simply should know what's happening. Simply pressing *send* is the answer for many managers, but it is an exceptionally ineffective method for communication.

b. People believe communication is happening simply because people talk.

c. And people believe communication is happening because things *seem* to be getting done.

> "I taught Performance Management to a group of service supervisors and managers a few times. When it came to performance management and particularly PIPs, I would ask, 'Are you absolutely sure that your employee is crystal clear on what you expect of them?' The answer most of the time was either 'no' or 'they ought to know.'"
>
> —Dr. Don Kirkey

d. Managers believe that people have ESP about managerial expectations.

Barrier #8: There is an invisible barrier of miscommunication between upper management and the rest of the organization.

Quite often, executives will have a clear sense of where *they're* going, and put together a communication plan for the organization. Yet people in the trenches often have no idea what's happening. There's a strange disconnect somewhere around the middle-management level where communication seems to vaporize. It's true in every organization I've worked with the past three decades, and it has a heavy influence on Organizational Engagement.

90   Rummler, G., & Brache, A. (1995). *Improving performance: How to manage the white space on the organization chart.* San Francisco: John Wiley & Sons, Inc.

Barrier #9: The organization is missing a feedback loop.

There is no effective feedback loop for employees and teams to address issues. The invisible communication barrier prevents communication from getting to and from the source. Finally, ensure the organization has effective communication feedback loops.

Barrier #10: For an individual to be effective, he or she must know the results of their actions.

Organizations must know how they are performing to increase Organizational Engagement. Feedback is critical. Thus, when organizations are performing well, they need to pass this information on to their constituents to increase organizational engagement. [91] Pritchard, et al. (1988) demonstrated that feedback (reporting the results of performance) is an extremely effective way of modifying behavior."[92] Thompson and Luthans (1990) state that feedback is necessary to enhance performance. "For example, when the employee does an outstanding job and management does not respond, there is no reinforcement of that level of effort. When management does not address poor performance, employees have no clear view of an acceptable level of performance. Only when management responds to particular levels of performance is there a connection made between performance behaviors and management desires."[93]

From the perspective of communication in Organizational Engagement, feedback represents the knowledge that a performance was accomplished. Every time leaders inform their organizations of achievement, they increase organizational momentum and engagement. Feedback on Performance Accomplishments is a component of communication that enhances Organizational Engagement.

---

[91]　p.99
[92]　p. 355
[93]　p. 325

Things that influence effective communication

Communicator	Communicatee
Speed of processing	Listening effectiveness
Sound bites	Timing of communication
Lack of patience	Physical space of communication
Clarity of sender	Distractions

What psychology tells us: the *individual* level of communication

Each person has a preferred way of communicating

Communication starts with individuals with varying degrees of motivation to converse and share information. Each person is a bit different in their approach to communication: some are more gregarious, some are restrained. Yet organizations must find ways to strengthen communication if they want to increase the level of Organizational Engagement.

Some barriers to individual communication

The primary barrier to effective communication is what's called "Willingness to communicate" (WTC).[94] "Whether a person is willing or not willing to communicate, either in a given circumstance or more generally, is a volitional choice which is cognitively processed."[95] Getting people to communicate means developing a willingness on their part to share information. You may have heard the phrase "knowledge is power." This idea, unfortunately, encourages people to hoard information in the perception that it makes them irreplaceable. In truth, *sharing* knowledge is the real source of power. That takes leadership effort.

---

94   McCroskey & Richmond, 1985
95   Booth-Butterfield, M. 1990. Communication, Cognition and Anxiety. J Soc Beh and Personality, Vol. (5), 2, 19-37.

Here's why people might be <u>unwilling</u> to communicate:[96]

▶ **Communication avoidance because of mistrust**

Talking only as much as is absolutely required. This is generally done out of fear or hiding something, possibly because of mistrust. Consider a meeting where people are deeply cautious about sharing information because of who is in the room.

▶ **Communication avoidance for fear of reactions**

Reluctance to tell people about a big change for fear of their reaction. This is no different than your kid not wanting to tell you about a bad report card. Again, think about how people avoid communicating because of what might happen to them in a large corporate meeting.

▶ **Communication withdrawal for self-protection**

Saying very little, if anything, about a situation. Think of the employee who knows something but is afraid of losing their job if they say anything.

It is up to good leaders to manage these issues. The point is this: Communication takes *effort*. It is not simply a given.

Ineffective communication has a negative impact on change initiatives

Communication issues don't only show up in individuals. In another study with graduate students in different markets (healthcare, non-profits, education, business, misc.), I asked, "What are the barriers to effective change?" Again, communication was number one.

---

96   Non-verbal communication is still manifested, so leaders must be attentive.

Chart 7. Barriers to change initiatives

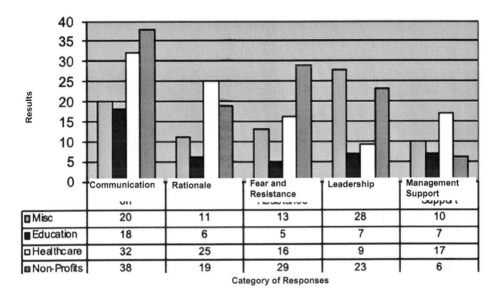

	Communication	Rationale	Fear and Resistance	Leadership	Management Support
▣ Misc	20	11	13	28	10
▪ Education	18	6	5	7	7
▫ Healthcare	32	25	16	9	17
▨ Non-Profits	38	19	29	23	6

Category of Responses

Structured Interview Results Barriers to Change in Organizations

We can see from Chart 7 that, irrespective of market, communication is the number-one barrier to change efforts, with healthcare and nonprofits being the most highly reported in this study, followed by Rationale (Healthcare) and Leadership (Misc and Business).

In yet another Graduate class study, from hundreds of structured interviews across scores of organizations, Communication is consistently the # 1 barrier to change in organizations! The primary reason? Organizations don't address the emotional complexity of change:

> "Organizations will benefit where the prevalent idea of communication as a rational process is dispelled…. It is the extent to which an organization can create either processes or habits that contain the complexities of emotion and relations that will make the difference to their ability to both acknowledge and utilize them in relation to learning and change."[97]

---

97   Vince, "The impact of Emotion on organizational learning," *Human Resource Development International* 5:1, 2002, 73-85, 83.

"Leaders who take organizational conversation seriously know when to stop talking and start listening. Few behaviors enhance conversational intimacy as much as attending to what people say. True attentiveness signals respect for people of all ranks and roles, a sense of curiosity, and even a degree of humility."[98]

As you can see, communication is critical but it takes serious effort!

Communication is the third major element of Organizational Engagement.

If people (1) know where they're going (2) can work together, and (3) have effective communication that keeps the organization informed, you're well on your way to increasing organizational engagement.

The **B**ohn **O**rganizational **E**ngagement **S**cale [BOES] includes four questions that focus on **COMMUNICATION.**

Employee Engagement and the Employee Experience do not address the element of organizational level communication. Here's why:

Employee engagement is focused exclusively on the employee's individual experience. While communication may be important, EE does not ask how an organization is sharing key information that is critical to the daily functioning of the enterprise.

The Employee Experience is a direct result of organizational communication, for without knowledge of what's happening, people follow the rumor mill and develop a wait-and-see attitude until someone fills in the blanks via communication, ultimately wasting their time and effort.

---

98   HBR *Leadership Is a Conversation* Boris Groysberg Michael Slind June 2012.

Now that you've had an opportunity to read through and think about communication, how would you rate your organization?

**<u>Not</u> focused on
Communication**

**Effectively managing
Communication**

ELEMENTS OF ORGANIZATIONAL ENGAGEMENT ANALYSIS

1. Do we know where we're going?

2. Can we work together?

3. Are we up to date with important information for our jobs?

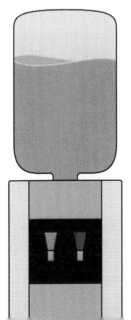

Chapter 10

Element #4: Conviction to persist—Resilience

Can we stay the course in the face of trouble?

REFLECTION QUESTIONS:

When people stand at the water cooler in your organization, how confident will they be that your company will endure in a crisis?

This fourth element of Organizational Engagement activates motivation by assuring individuals the organization has the staying power and conviction to endure when things get tough.

Any endeavor that holds the promise of a meaningful and influential achievement requires persistence. The word *persistence* evokes images of both frustration and heroism. *Frustration*, because persistence in the face of struggle strikes us as costly; *heroism*, because we know that the greater the challenge, the greater the glory in achieving something monumental.

Acknowledging the sages of the ages

Clearly, history is filled with amazing achievements with some, like cathedrals, that took centuries of persistence to build... Others, like the great social justice movements, are hallmarks of the human pursuit of equity. Those stories, biographies, and anecdotes are beyond the scope of this book but they remind us of *the importance of resilience*. This section is about the more mundane, yet important element of persistence in the workplace.

Conviction is workplace persistence

Without workplace conviction, many projects are started, but few are completed. It happens all the time.

1. Executives come up with new and fanciful ideas, but they lack the will to complete them. *Conviction makes ideas reality.*

2. Strategic planning sessions take place with great aplomb, only to languish on the shelves as dusty three-ring binders. *Conviction turns planning into action.*

3. Barriers arise that drain the heart and soul from technology teams, product delivery groups, and innovators. *Conviction helps teams overcome setbacks.*

4. Executive support dries up for once desirable projects. *Conviction shows people that boredom is not an acceptable work ethic.*

As businesspeople know, these situations are not at all that unusual. In fact, they're common among diverse markets, geographies, and technologies. It's interesting that strategic plans, new products, and once-desirable projects were once held in high esteem. So, completing these initiatives must still have value. Will they get done? It's a question of conviction. Conviction, ultimately, is about a willingness to endure short term pain for long term gain.

Practical tip: Conviction at the individual level: how is it developed?

I suppose the short answer is: "*Persist!*" But that's not helpful, so what are some practical ways people develop persistence?

1. Exercise, which teaches the mind to overcome bodily discomfort

2. Learning something complex (a language or chess)

3. Learning a musical instrument requires significant persistence. Mastering a musical instrument requires decades of practice.

4. Learning to manage physical discomfort in the office setting (long meetings require significant self-discipline to maintain concentration).

5. Learning to concentrate during conversations you'd rather not be part of

6. Managing boredom through creative time management (what do you do to redeem the time? There is always something to do to overcome boredom.)

7. Managing waiting, in places like doctor's offices, governmental agencies, inefficient stores, even waiting online or on the phone

---

Individual resilience provides insight into organizational conviction.

The psychology of individual resilience

In a 2002 article, Diane Coutu wrote:

"Most of the resilience theories I encountered in my research make good common sense. But I also observed that almost all the theories overlap in three ways. Resilient people, they posit, possess three characteristics: a staunch acceptance of reality; a deep belief, often buttressed by strongly held values, that life is meaningful; and an uncanny ability to improvise. You can bounce back from hardship with just one or two of these qualities, but you will only be truly resilient with all three. These three characteristics hold true for resilient organizations as well."[99]

To paraphrase Coutu, understanding that hard times can impact an organization, and knowing an organization has a meaningful mission, and developing the ability to improvise, manifests itself in organizational resilience.

Let's look at what clinicians tell us builds individual resilience and then use their insights to explain how it works in corporations. We know people can learn to be resilient by successfully managing complex and demanding experiences. Resilience takes time and effort. It is something positive that comes out of something negative. [100] It is a sense of coping with difficult events by means of the following:

Flexibility: The skill of "rolling with the punches," accepting that things did not go well, but working our way through them anyway.

Supportive relationships: Having others work through an issue with us, giving us advice and encouragement along the way.

Learning: Learning allows us to glean useful knowledge from a bad experience.

Capacity for developing plans: By developing plans, individuals find their way out of difficult and demanding circumstances.

Communication: Talking about a situation and clarifying it allows people to build resilience by managing through the circumstances and sharing the emotional stresses.

The ability to manage intense feelings and impulses: Resilience is demonstrated when people manage fear and impulses that arise because of past trauma.

---

99   https://hbr.org/2002/05/how-resilience-works, Diane Coutu
100 Condensed from Gerry Miller, *Learning the language of addiction counseling*, 267–69.

Each of these behaviors has an <u>organizational-level equivalent</u>:

Flexibility: Leaders can help people adjust to change and challenges by shifting resources to more critical areas of an organization. This is the ability to 'roll with the punches' of market distress and unexpected challenges.

Supportive relationships: Offering resources and assistance to departments which are struggling can make a major difference in their success.

Learning: Leaders can take advantage of learning to help people adjust. What leaders learn about resilience can be shared.

Capacity for developing plans: When things go wrong, organizations regroup and shift their resources to plan corrective actions.

Communication: Bringing specific issues to the surface with honesty and clarity and *without fear of retaliation* goes a long way in developing conviction.

The ability to manage intense feelings and impulses: Strong leaders help organizations get through the toughest times by managing their own fear.

Conviction at the Organizational Level

Organizational Engagement theory explains that when people are facing genuine obstacles or impediments to progress at work, they can sense whether their organization will be able to persist and overcome or simply give up. At the individual level, resilience is the ability to overcome difficulties and stay the course when things go wrong.[101] If a person senses imminent doom when things go wrong, they most likely do not have enough motivation to persist. If people sense that their organization is not going to succeed, they withdraw. They spend their time at the water cooler discussing their frustrations and speculating about what—or who—will fail next. Just when the organization needs their efforts the most, a vicious downward spiral begins.

Organizations that do not have the conviction to stay the course during times of trouble will not likely survive. Tom Lowery, the president of Building Controls at Legrand Holdings uses the phrase "strategic discipline" for staying the course in the face of obstacles.[102]

---

101 Bandura, 1997.
102 Tom Lowery, personal conversation, May 2019

At the individual level, people sense their loss of an ability to control an outcome and become anxious.[103] We know a person's sense of anxiety can negatively influence their ability to control outcomes. The ability to overcome anxiety is resilience, a key factor in human success. It is especially critical after people have endured a trauma. This is also true in organizations.

Conviction—resilience—is the ability to stay the course.

An organization strong in engagement will have a powerful sense of resilience. Kotter and Heskett (1992) describe a strong organization in the following way: "There is a feeling of shared confidence: the members believe, without a doubt, *that they can effectively manage whatever new problems and opportunities come their way.*"[104] Ryan and Oestrich, in their insightful work on fear in the workplace, note that "fear's cost largely comes down to figuring the influence of negative emotions on people's work and how it affects the potential of individuals and the organization as a whole."[105] They recognize that fear has a negative impact on organizational performance, which drains effectiveness. Thus, an organization must develop conviction and resilience to overcome the impact of fear.

Larson and LaFasto (1989) state:

> "When strong technical skills are combined with a desire to contribute and an ability to be collaborative, the observable outcome is an elevated sense of confidence among team members. This confidence (engagement?), in turn, translates into the ability of a team to be self-correcting in *its capacity to adjust to unexpected adversity and emergent challenges.*"[106]

Adjusting to "adversity and emergent challenges" is precisely what we would expect in an organization high in organizational engagement. Resilience—conviction—means getting up more times than we are knocked down.[107] Conviction is the ability to stay the course in the face of obstacles.

---

103 Maddux, 1995.
104 p. 45
105 Ryan & Oestrich , 1998, p. 107
106 p. 71 – italics mine
107 Diane Coutu *Harvard Business Review* 2002.

Conviction is critical for long-term organizational success

I recall an executive once telling my former organization, "People should not see our shoulders fall." That was an expression of conviction to persist—resilience.

Resilience is especially critical in adoption of organizational change. Organizations that can accept and embrace the difficulties inherent in change are more likely to rapidly integrate new concepts and technologies into the organization, outpacing competition. Resilience is a sense of flexibility, of bouncing back from tough setbacks. It is the ability to move forward, *changing a tire on a moving bus*, so to speak. Resilient organizations adopt new ideas quickly.

Organizations that feel overwhelmed by their competitors or sense that everything is falling apart are not likely to have a strong sense of Organizational Engagement. While there are many reasons for this, a sense of dread that pervades an organization will deplete its strength. A sense of resilience is that capability to bounce back in the face of these obstacles and trials.

Ways organizations can increase resilience:

1. Organizations can increase a sense of resilience by articulating the future, or, in the case of serious setbacks, pointing out the light at the end of the tunnel, and it is up to *leaders to show the way.*

2. Strategic planning builds resilience because it helps people see where a company is going.

3. Clarity of direction builds resilience because it helps people know how things will get done.

4. Knowledge of achievements builds resilience because people see what their organization is accomplishing. Past achievements have one powerful value: "We've done this before, we've weathered hard storms before."

5. Increasing innovation to develop creative and cutting-edge concepts that will grow into new product lines.

6. Increasing revenue by winning large contracts is another means of building resilience.

Additional means for increasing resilience

Communicating Performance Accomplishments increase Resilience

"Look at what we did."

- Completion of major projects
- Inventions
- Awards
- Publications of Organizational Success
- Performance Reports
- Sales accomplishments (being awarded large contracts)
- Communicating Effective Reengineering projects
- Sales Performance
- History of the company
- Acquisition of other businesses

The key to building resilience is communicating successes effectively at the employee level, so people continue to gain confidence in their future.

The **B**ohn **O**rganizational **E**ngagement **S**cale [BOES] includes four questions that focus on **CONVICTION.**

Employee Engagement and the Employee Experience do not address the element of Resilience. Here's why:

Employee engagement is focused exclusively on the individual experience of the employee does not ask questions that address resilience in the context of the organization. It does not assess whether people believe an organization is going to survive, a critical element in motivation.

The Employee Experience is a direct result of organizational conviction - resilience, for without a strong level of confidence that their organization will survive the storms of business, people will be uncomfortable, anxious, unproductive and likely looking for new jobs.

Now that you've had an opportunity to read through and think about resilience, how would you rate your organization?

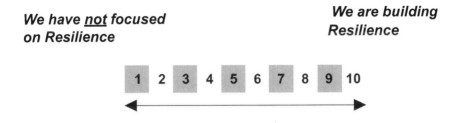

*We have **not** focused on Resilience*

We are building Resilience

1 2 3 4 5 6 7 8 9 10

ELEMENTS OF ORGANIZATIONAL ENGAGEMENT ANALYSIS

1. *Do we know where we're going?*

2. *Can we work together?*

3. *Are we up to date with important information for our jobs?*

4. *Can we stay the course when things get tough?*

Chapter 11

Element #5: Leadership Commitment
Do we have confidence that our leadership gets things done?

REFLECTION QUESTIONS:

When people stand at the water cooler in your organization, how confident are they in the leadership of the company? Could they say, without a doubt, they know the leadership gets things done and has great follow-through? Or would they say, "I'm not really sure"?

This fifth element of organizational engagement motivates employees by ensuring them that their leadership has a clear path to success. In short, employees believe their leaders can get things done.

Leadership is endlessly studied for good reason: it is the lynchpin for all organizational success, the executive system in the organizational brain that brings all the parts together. Chemers wrote, "Leadership is the 'executive function' of organizational intelligence. Leaders must establish and encourage norms, roles, and rules for efficient application to known tasks, but must also be sensitive and responsive to change by employing sensitivity, problem solving, and decision-making strategies that allow for adaptation." [108] Executives are faced with chaotic situations and complex issues with no clear boundaries. This is the true test of leadership, and this is where true leaders shine. Great executives have the ability to bring order out of chaos.[109]

Leaders manage the tough stuff: VUCA—Volatility, Uncertainty,

---

108 Chemers, M. M. (1997). *An integrative theory of leadership.* Mahwah, NJ: Lawrence Elrbaum Associates.

109 Giles, S. (2018, May 9). "How VUCA is reshaping the business environment, and what it means for innovation," *Forbes.* Retrieved from https://www.forbes.com/sites/sunniegiles/2018/05/09/how-vuca-is-reshaping-the-business-environment-and-what-it-means-for-innovation/#ef20102eb8d5

Complexity and Ambiguity

VUCA is an acronym developed by the students of the U.S. Army War College. These days, most executives acknowledge that their organizations operate in an environment that is Volatile, Uncertain, Complex, and Ambiguous. That's when their true leadership ability shines. There is no doubt that leaders influence organizations: "Research on managerial succession over the last 20 years has consistently found a relationship between who is in charge and organizational performance." Estimates ranging from 14% to 45% of an organization's effectiveness are ascribed to leadership.[110]

While researchers agree that leaders' influence is universal, it is important that we precisely articulate exactly what leadership is doing to influence organizational engagement.

Below are the results of a quick poll I conducted with a group of nearly fifty leaders in multiple organizations.

The one thing that gives me confidence an organization can accomplish its goals is... they could answer multiple times (N=44)

Table 7. Confidence that an organization can accomplish desired goals

OPEN-ENDED RESPONSE	STAFF, ACADEMICS, N=22	MIDDLE MANAGEMENT N=13	EXECUTIVES N=9
Leadership	24%	38%	50%
Commitment, Constancy, Focus	24%	15%	25%
Teamwork (coworkers)	4% 16%	8%	25%
Track Record	16%	8%	12%
Vision	0%	0%	25%
Goals	12%	46%	12%

110 Kaiser, Hogan and Craig, 2008. p. 103

Leadership takes first place as a major influence in organizations.

Table 7 shows us that leadership is top of mind as influencing organizational effectiveness. And employees have perceptions *about their belief in leadership effectiveness for controlling outcomes.*[111]

Author after author after author remind us of the key organizational influence of leadership, sometimes to excess— we hear of Navy Seal Leadership, servant leadership, and numerous other examples.

Leadership is the guidance system for the organization.

Katz and Kahn, in their famous work, *The Social Psychology of Organizations*, wrote: "In the description of organizations, no word is more often used than leadership, and perhaps no word is used with such varied meanings. Leadership is sometimes used as if it were an attribute of personality, sometimes as if it were a characteristic of certain positions, and sometime as an attribute of behavior."[112]

Leadership has even been identified as a source of organizational energy: "Organizational energy is related but not identical to the sum of the energy of individuals. Individual energy, especially of leaders, influences organizational energy, and the energy state of the organization affects the energy of individuals."[113] Organizational energy, while interesting, is vague and difficult to measure; nonetheless, the concept tells us that leaders are providing the fuel for organizational success.

Leadership literature continues to expand, yet it does not answer a key question: *How are leaders assessed in the minds of followers?* How much do followers believe leaders truly influence their organizations? And in what ways? And what impact does that assessment of leader effectiveness have on the motivation of individuals?

Here's the contribution of Leadership to Organizational Engagement

Followers have a collective sense of whether their leadership is about words getting things done. Leadership influences Organizational Engagement by providing direction and communication. Research also shows that upper-level leadership has a strong correlation to the collective power of the organization[114]. Upper level leaders influence how followers perceived organizational engagement.

---

111   Byrne, 2015

112   Katz, D., & Kahn, R. L. (1978). *The social psychology of organizations* (2nd ed.). New York: Wiley.p. 574

113   Bruch, and Ghoshal, p. 45.

114   Chen, G. & Bliese, P. (2002). The role of different levels of leadership in predicting self and collective efficacy: evidence for discontinuity. Journal of Applied Psychology. 87, (3), 549- 556.

My work with leaders

I have raised the issue of leadership effectiveness through decades of work with hundreds of leaders. Whether I've spoken with them, observed them, or reported to them, several themes of effective leadership emerged. By consolidating theory, interviews, surveys, and sentence completion exercises into a framework of leader behavior, I arrived at these key elements of Leadership: **Vision, Persistence, Personal Belief in their ability to get things done, Communication,** and **Validated Accomplishments** (track record). These elements are confirmed by even a cursory reading of management literature.

Vision

Connecting with the first element of Organizational Engagement, Mission, we know that leaders are responsible for developing a compelling vision. Griffen, et. al. write, "Our findings suggest that leaders can motivate more proactivity and adaptively... by presenting a clear, compelling, and discrepant view of the future."[115]That means leaders have a sense of what could be and how to get there. Further, "A strong leader vision challenges employees to help change the organization, and employees who have high levels of role-breadth self-efficacy *respond to this challenge* by actively helping to bring about the change."[116] Decades of leadership literature is loaded with the notion that leaders establish a vision. *But that's not enough. And people know it.* Here's why:

> "Leaders are often good at one activity ... creating a vision, but rarer is the leader who can integrate and relentlessly pursue all the essential components of change."[117]

Persistence

While leadership vision may be important, persistence to achieve the vision is just as important. As noted in Chapter 4 – Conviction, leaders influence long-term persistence. "In the early stages of a leader-follower relationship, judgments of these characteristics are based on image and impression, but, as time goes by, they are based on experience and evaluation."[118] As employees consider Organizational Engagement, they ask themselves, "Do our leaders persist in the face of struggle, despair or obstacles?

---

115 p. 180, Griffin, Parker and Mason.

116 P. 176

117 Miller, D. *Journal of Change Management,* December 2001 2:4, 359-368

118 Chemers, M. M., Watson, C. B., & May, S. T. (2000). "Dispositional affect and leadership effectiveness: A comparison of self-esteem, optimism, and efficacy." *Personality and Social Psychology Bulletin,* 26(3), 267-277.

Personal belief in their ability to get things done

Leaders know whether they can get things done—in academic terms, they have a sense of their own efficacy to bring about success. Chemers, et al., conducted research in the military and developed a scale for self-perception of efficacy in leadership skills. They included such items as "I am confident in my ability to influence the group I lead," and "I know what it takes to make a group accomplish its task."[119] Follower perceptions mirror their leader's self-perception, and thus are a component of Organizational Engagement.

Communication

Developing a vision is important, but the leader that does not interact effectively with team members is unlikely to be successful. Leaders are effective communicators. In Griffin, Parker, Mason cite the "ability to communicate..." as a key factor in organizational success.[120] Although communication is an exceptionally broad term, followers understand how well (or poorly) their leaders communicate new ideas, instructions, recognition, and expectations. The details are mentioned in Chapter 9 on communication, but they are worth repeating, because leader communication is the glue that holds everything together.

Validated Accomplishments (Track Record)

Leaders who lack a successful track record will not gain the support they need from followers and thus diminish Organizational Engagement. Do leaders have a history of accomplishment that others can point to with confidence in future achievement? Do leaders get things done? "Without credibility, there is no leadership."[121] Credibility is gained through outcomes, achievements, which are ultimately a result of getting people to work together.

---

119 Chemers, et al, (2000).

120 Ng,K., Ang, S., & Chan, K. (2008) "Personality and leader effectiveness: a moderated mediation model of leadership self-efficacy, job demands, and job autonomy." *Journal of Applied Psychology* 2008, 93 (4): 733-43.

121 Chemers, 1997.

Again, Leadership expert Chemers explains:

> "Leadership is a process of social influence. For leaders to exert influence, followers must accept and respond to the leader's persuasion. Followers make the decision about whether an individual should be accorded leadership status by comparing a leader's presented characteristics or image against deeply held assumptions about what constitutes a credible leader. The two characteristics that are most central to these expectations are task-relevant competence and trustworthiness. In the early stages of a leader-follower relationship, judgments of these characteristics are based on image and impression, but as time goes by, they are based on experience and evaluation. Without credibility, there is no leadership."[122]

Although it may be common sense to most of us in organizations, this chapter reminds us that leadership is a critical element of organizational engagement.[123]

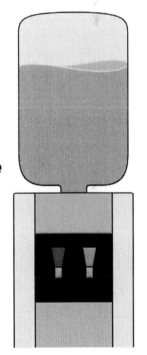

"Soft skills" do not exist. Leading is the most demanding element of OE.

---

122 Chemers (1997).

123 Leadership influences organizational engagement. In a study of government officials in New Zealand, Leadership contributed significantly to prediction of organizational engagement over and above what the demographics (age, time in the job, gender) could predict (R^2 change = .128, F Change (3, 157) =16.62, p <.001). Thus, the Leadership variable set uniquely accounted for 13% of the variance of organizational engagement.

Dr. Bohn's perspective on leadership

In addition to the works listed above, I wanted to add my own perspective on leadership after working with literally hundreds of leaders, both strong and weak.

Though there are numerous books on what I call the "technology of leadership," —the process of delegation, the nuances of managing finance and data, and the constant effort to properly structure an organization to achieve strategic goals—little is written about the leader as an artist.

The structure provided by the technician is extremely important, but never enough.

As I continue to listen to leaders who have achieved much in their lifetimes, I hear more than technology. I hear artistry. The more I hear about employee engagement, transparency, and authenticity, the more I hear artistry. The more the millennial generation asks for coaching, interaction, and mentoring, the more I hear artistry.

Why? Because artists sense the world in a deep way. Because artists find connections between things that are not always obvious. Because artists are far more tuned into people.

Don't get me wrong, I understand the need for the "technology of leadership," because focusing exclusively on people inevitably leads to a country club atmosphere where stuff just doesn't get done. The structure provided by the technicians is extremely important, but never enough. I'll wager the majority of great leaders have some artist in their blood.

The leader as artist taps creativity

The leader as artist trusts their intuition to develop solutions. The leader as artist uses creativity to solve problems. The artist seeks out and delights in innovation. The art of leadership is found in applying creativity in solutions, looking beyond the "tried and true" and seeking a way to bring all the parts together in an elegant composition. In this way, the leader is an artist.

The leader as artist engages human emotion

Emotional intelligence is ultimately artistry because artists understand human emotion better than the general population. I'll admit, sometimes artists wear their emotions on their sleeve, but the point is that emotion is part of artistry. Emotion is a sense of awareness of what's going on between people.

The leader as artist reads the room.

I've met few "technician leaders" who have a sense of when people have run out of energy, are bored, or need a quick break. Technician leaders just keep driving, no matter how tired the team is. That may work in the military, but it is a bad strategy in the workplace. Leader artists have a sense of when people are not as attentive as they could be, just like an artist or musician reads a room to sense when to shift energy or focus.

Reading a room requires adapting to the moment instead of simply charging through with the agenda. So many leaders who are technicians are focused exclusively on a task, and they forget the people who need to complete those tasks. The leader as artist perceives something wrong and acts to make course corrections.

The leader as artist grasps the big picture.

Organizational problems often require assembling the motivation of many to gain something bigger. This is artistry. This is where the leader assesses his or her B and C players and thinks, *I can get more from them; they have more to offer.* And the leader as artist draws out (no pun intended) the capabilities and skills of those perceived as less helpful or useful simply by understanding what everyone can offer to a big problem.

Can this be taught?

I doubt that leadership artistry can be taught, except perhaps through modeling, since so much of this approach is an intrinsic part of a great leader. But even those 'leaders as technicians' can be wise and hire 'leaders as artists' into their teams and learn from them. The leader as artist is picking up things the technician will never see.

I'm convinced that the reason a major percentage of managerial people never become great leaders is because they're stalled at "technician" and likely to stay there—efficient but never able to transcend the basics.

Great leaders are artists.

The **B**ohn **O**rganizational **E**ngagement **S**cale [BOES] includes five questions that focus on **LEADERSHIP**[124]

Employee Engagement and the Employee Experience do not address the element of Leadership — here's why

Employee engagement is focused exclusively on the individual experience of the employee, and while the leadership effectiveness of the organization may be important to an individual, EE is focused very locally (the immediate supervisor) and does not ask questions that address leadership effectiveness *in the context of the organization.* Although there are questions about supervision, the overarching context of organizational leadership effectiveness is not addressed by employee engagement.

The Employee Experience is a direct result of organizational leadership, for the people who design the organizational strategy and provide day-to-day coaching have the greatest impact on employee lives – far more than any perk a company has to offer.

---

124 Alpha level for the 5-item leadership scale was .93 for 589 cases. The one factor solution (LEADERSHIP) accounted for 79% of the variance, with an Eigenvalue of 3.944.

Now that you've had an opportunity to read through and think about leadership, how would you rate your organization?

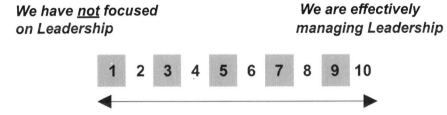

We have <u>not</u> focused on Leadership

We are effectively managing Leadership

1 2 3 4 5 6 7 8 9 10

ELEMENTS OF ORGANIZATIONAL ENGAGEMENT ANALYSIS

1. **Do we know where we're going?**

2. **Can we work together?**

3. **Are we up to date with important information for our jobs?**

4. **Can we stay the course when things get tough?**

5. **Are our leaders credible and do they get things done?**[125]

---

125 The subject of leadership has been an ongoing discussion for decades (Kotter, 1990; Truske, 1999; Posner & Kouzes, 1987; Bennis, 1989; Bennis & Nanus, 1985) and has roots as far back as 1921 (Hughes, Ginnett & Curphy, 1999, p. 8). It is considered an essential component of Industrial and Organizational Psychology (Howell & Dipboye, 1982, pp. 125-176). The power of charismatic leadership has been examined and challenged (Nadler & Tushman, 1990), leadership is considered an essential component of powerful organizational cultures (Kotter & Heskett, 1992), and there have been works on emotional intelligence and leadership (Cooper & Sawaf, 1996; Goleman, 1998). The literature is immense.

Chapter 12

Element #6: Consequences

Are people held accountable for their work?

REFLECTION QUESTIONS:

In human experience, nothing is more important over the long haul than a belief that one has been treated fairly.

When people stand at the water cooler in your organization, are they convinced that your organization has a culture of accountability? Do they believe your organization plays fair? Does the organization reward and promote fairly? Is your organization focusing energy on the right things, or is it wasting employees' precious time? Do people believe you reward excellence and remove mediocrity?

This sixth and final element of organizational engagement activates motivation by reassuring individuals that their organization has a sense of accountability, justice, and fairness.

Memories of unfairness rarely fade

Ever notice that people remember bad things that have been done to them in organizations? People have long memories of unfairness and mistreatment. People rarely overlook favoritism in management. People do not forget unfair practices. They're no different than the child who laments, "That's not fair!"

The impact of accountability on organizations

We spend a lot of time discussing and improving the fundamentals of business including organizational financials—*profit and loss, income statements, return on investment, revenue, and balance sheets*. We spend a lot of time training leaders how to lead and managers how to manage. We spend a lot of time on product development, innovation, entrepreneurial actions and marketing concepts. But how much time do we spend talking about organizational *accountability*?

What does accountability mean in the context of organizations? At the ground level it means, "I want to clearly understand how my performance is measured. Are there rewards for good performance and consequences for bad performance? I want to know people are held accountable for the quality of their work."

Consequences—accountability—is far more than checking the box of compliance.

For some of you, accountability brings to mind the standard, mandatory ethics policies organizations bring out every year requiring compliance. This is a check-the-box activity. People must agree to the ethics statements or they're fired. But I'm not talking about those check-the-box actions. I'm talking about the actual concept—a philosophy, if you will—of accountability. It is an overlooked link in organizational performance.

Accountability: rarely discussed, yet critical to performance

A great challenge for organizations in the years ahead

Businesses work hard to enhance organizations by improving product offerings, product quality, and ROI. They engage customer focus groups and do all that is needed to achieve the financial elements of good business. Yet, in the years ahead, as the millennial generation takes over corporate leadership, one of the greatest challenges we have will be an improvement in organizational accountability. And it is likely to be some of the hardest, soul-searching change organizations undertake.

Accountability: we don't talk about it, but we should.

Even though organizations may have a strong and well-known mission, communicate effectively and have good leadership capacity, people may still be deeply aware of things that seem unfair or wrong. These injustices corrode organizational engagement, but they are often overlooked by leadership in the name of profitability. Employees tell and retell the legends of organizational failures and how people have not been held accountable for poor work, product failures, or worse.

OE Theory includes accountability because people have a deep sense of how their organization manages consequences both good and bad. Consequences are well known in organizations, ranging from great successes to miserable failures. People know whether *and how* their organizations hold people accountable, which influences motivation. Accountability is a critical element of OE.

What is accountability? Let's break that down.

Accountability can be a simple thing, like following up and keeping one's word, or a complex thing, like reward and recognition, promotions, treatment of minorities, along with fair and equitable distribution of perks and other amenities. But it is much, much more. Let's take this a level deeper and analyze accountability at a deep and granular level.

Learning about accountability from, well, accountants!

Accountability is one of those odd words we toss about randomly, believing that we and others share the same definition. *(Generally, it means we hope someone gets caught for doing something they should <u>not</u> be doing, right?)* But I'm not sure we have a clear definition of accountability in organizations. So, in deference to those careful and logical souls who hold the world's businesses *accountable*, let's take a page out of their notebook and apply their concepts to organizational behavior. *Let's learn about accountability from **accountants**.*

1. Accountability is accuracy

Our workplaces rely on accuracy. For example, data must be correct, or our systems fail. The decisions we make require accuracy. I like to say, *The angels are in the details,* for that is where truth presents itself. Accuracy requires effort, patience, persistence, and a thoughtful review of all the facts. *Managers and leaders who don't sweat the details find themselves losing credibility in the short run, because, in the long run, the numbers matte—and unless they're fudged, the numbers don't lie.* Any forensic accountant will tell you that the numbers eventually tell the story.

Organizational Engagement relies on <u>accuracy</u>, because accuracy is transparency, and transparency builds trust, the ultimate source of organizational effectiveness.

2. Accuracy is completeness.

Half-truths do not serve organizations very well. When there are issues that must be brought to the surface, yet remain hidden for personal or political reasons, we sometimes do not have a complete picture of a situation. In most cases, a lack of completeness has minimal impact on a situation (maybe some rework or frustration in the ranks), but in other cases, incomplete data can have catastrophic consequences. Just ask any leader of a major ERP (Enterprise Relationship Management) project. *Managers and leaders who present incomplete pictures of their situation to protect themselves from career damage can run, but they cannot hide. I've seen some managers get in serious trouble because they only presented part of a story to shield themselves from trouble.*

Organizational Engagement relies on <u>completeness</u>, because completeness is thoroughness, which, again, builds trust, the ultimate source of organizational effectiveness.

3. Accounting is consistency

GAAP (Generally Accepted Accounting Principles) apply everywhere. There's a reason. The language and definition of the numbers must be consistent to allow global transactions that carry common meaning. Integrity means consistency in management and leadership. We cannot say one thing and do something completely different in our behavior. *This issue has become even more prominent with increasing employee expectations for transparency.*

Organizational Engagement relies on <u>consistency</u>, because consistency means people aren't guessing, which builds trust, the ultimate source of organizational effectiveness.

4. Accounting reveals the truth

Within the past several years, the world has seen situation after situation arise where, because of forensic accounting practices, the *truth shows up.* It is so strange to this author that, in a world of millisecond transactions (when I post a blog it becomes globally live in billionths of a second and part of a public record), leaders and managers somehow believe that they can cut corners or hide information. *Because the truth eventually comes out.*

Organizational Engagement relies on <u>truth</u>, because truth builds trust, the ultimate source of organizational effectiveness.

5. Accounting eventually means an audit

Managerial and leadership behavior is constantly on display. Our employees audit us every day. Our peers audit us. Our managers audit us. Our communities audit us. There is no soft-pedaling this issue. And with instantaneous access through social media, nothing remains hidden very long. The global audit happens one way or another. *Secrecy does not bode well with accountants.*

Organizational Engagement relies on the fact that an audit will eventually take place, and there is nothing to hide.

Here's how employees view accountability in organizations:

1. The abuse of power has the greatest impact on perceptions of accountability.

Organizations that permit bullying and abuse within their ranks degrade organizational engagement, because employees will not trust an organization that ignores, permits, or even encourages the abuse of power.

2. Reputation and mythology may skew the notion of accountability.

It is true that one or two stories of leadership failures can become the prevailing mythology about an organization, and thus people can develop a skewed view of a company. Nonetheless, employees do have a sense of unfairness, especially in cases where they feel someone "got away with it."

3. Accountability builds trust in the organization and its leadership.

Follow-through on projects builds trust in the organization. People develop trust in leaders who see a project through to completion. Trust is built when communication is high—people know what's happening and why. Trust in the organization is built when people, *especially top leadership*, keep their word. A sense of organizational justice reduces employee uncertainty and increases perceptions of trustworthiness.[126]

4. Accountability influences employee commitment to change.

In a study of justice and organizational change by Rex Foster, "results revealed that employees who perceived high levels of fairness associated with an organizational change were *more likely to want to be committed to the change* (**affective**), more likely to *feel that they ought to be committed to the change* (**normative**) and *less likely to be committed to the change because of perceived costs* (**continuance**)."[127] Fairness counts!

---

126 Foster, p. 13
127 Foster, R. (2010). "Resistance, Justice and Commitment to change." *Human Resource Development Quarterly*, 21, 1, Spring 2010. 3-39.

5. Accountability activates peer-to-peer motivation.

When peers see others held accountable, it influences their work for the good. When peers see others not held accountable for actions or incomplete projects or shoddy work, it does not go unnoticed and activates cynicism, skepticism and social loafing. We all have stories of people simply getting by and doing very little, whilst others work hard. The famous Q12[128] survey contains a question that reveals how we view the quality of others: "My associates are committed to doing quality work."

6. Accountability is demonstrated and acknowledged through rewards and recognition.

Verbal praise and coaching are forms of reward that demonstrate accountability for actions. Rewards and recognition play a role in increasing (or decreasing) a sense of *fair* accountability.

Perceptions of fairness are critical in organizational accountability.

Fairness is an element of accountability viewed 4 ways:

1. **Distributive Fairness: Are the outcomes or results fair?**

2. **Procedural Fairness: Is the process fair, consistent, and bias-free?**

3. **Informational Fairness: Are explanations provided?**

4. **Interpersonal Fairness: Are people treated fairly?**

---

128 Buckingham, M., & Coffman, C. (1999). *First, break all the rules: What the world's greatest managers do differently*. New York, NY: Simon & Schuster.

Perceptions of fairness in organizational behavior

1. Perceptions of accountability in hiring and firing

The process for hiring and firing demonstrates whether an organization treats people fairly, even when things have not worked out. Terminations, for example, carry legendary weight, largely because they happen infrequently and are often heard about (and sometimes feared) by everyone in the organization. Perceptions of fairness are critical in organizational accountability. Organizations that hold themselves accountable for effective and fair terminations increase perceptions of fairness. "Attention to justice in layoffs led to more favorable employee reactions to the outcomes."[129] Effective hiring practices also demonstrate accountability in fairness and due process.

2. Perceptions of fairness in the distribution of raises, promotions, and perks

Parking spaces, office spaces, and special treatment influence a perception of accountability. People are not unlike children who can perceive if something is out of balance. Travel policies, work-life balance, and other elements of fairness flow into accountability. Organizational Engagement is minimized when people consistently perceive unfairness.

3. Financial rewards have the greatest impact on accountability, risking perceptions of favoritism.

Compensation has the biggest impact of all on accountability. People who are financially rewarded for poor work, personality, or anything other than excellence in both profit and people causes harm to Organizational Engagement. And people watch this behavior: heavy financial rewards for poor performance are counterproductive at best and radically ignorant at worst, bordering on favoritism. Does your company treat some people as 'special' and above consequence because of their skillset?

---

129 Foster, p. 14

4. Breathing dinosaur projects influence a sense of accountability.

When old programs stay in place as the organization adds new initiatives, employees can become cynical, especially if those old programs are someone's pet project that continues to sap organizational strength, time, funding, and resources.

More programs and initiatives, while other old programs remain in place do not help an organization. When employees sense that no one is the air-traffic controller managing all the incoming projects, they lose confidence that someone is holding the organization accountable.

The primary focus of accountability in today's organizations: The management of HR interpersonal issues

Today, there is a focus of accountability in the areas of preventing sexual harassment and promoting diversity and inclusion. Even HR staff build reputations of fairness (or its opposite). Discrimination, harassment, and other elements of interpersonal HR fairness are part of accountability, but the details are well documented in other literature and beyond the scope of this book.

5. Accountability is degraded by perceptions of excessive organizational politics.

When employees feel that political maneuvering is more important than engineering, finance, legal, HR, or operations, they wonder about the effectiveness of accountability in an organization. If more effort is expended on managing coalitions and back room agreements than getting the actual work done, people become suspicious about the true intentions of their leaders.

6. Ultimately, people have an unwritten sense of accountability.

Executives could argue that employee perceptions of accountability could be skewed by some legendary disastrous experience in corporate history like a product failure where a leader didn't get fired. It is true that one or two stories of leadership failures can become the prevailing mythology about how an organization approaches accountability, and thus people can have a skewed view of a company. Nonetheless, employees do have a sense of fairness and reward. People have an unwritten and unexpressed sense of organizational accountability. It is very real.

The impact of accountability on organizations

What are the negative consequences of low perceived accountability? Degradation of OE through learned helplessness.

When achievements are unnoticed or unrecognized, people lose the desire to achieve more. This tendency is called *learned helplessness.* They will also feel they have been treated unfairly and are likely to remember this injustice for many years.

The resentment that people feel due to an injustice causes them to question motives of leadership, slowing down productivity and wasting time on evaluating decisions. For example, performance reviews that do not acknowledge achievement negatively impact those who have achieved much but have been recognized for little. Those are just a few aspects of organizational behavior companies should consider on their way to improved organizational accountability. Employees become distressed when poor workmanship is not addressed, because it demonstrates a lack of accountability.

Accountability is an essential element of Organizational Engagement.

Accountability is critical to organizational success. At its heart, accountability is philosophical—it's about justice and fairness, topics which rarely see the light of day in the popular organizational literature. Accountability is based on the trust employees place in their organizations. Accountability means maintaining the social contract (you employ me, and I'll do a good job). Accountability means not having excessive surveillance on individuals. Accountability means fair wages and fair promotions—in short, accountability means a lack of corruption in the organization.[130]

> "Research on organizational justice has shown that when people see themselves as being or having been treated fairly, they develop attitudes and behaviors associated with successful change.... However, when people experience an injustice or betrayal, they report resentment, a sense of being done to, and a desire for retribution, which can result in such negative behaviors as stealing, lower productivity, lower work quality, and less cooperation, along with the loss of trust, of obligation toward and satisfaction with their employer. "[131]

130 Kramer, R. (1999). "Trust and distrust in organizations: Emerging perspectives, Enduring questions." *Annual Review of Psychology,* 1999, 50(569-598).

131 Ford, J., Ford, L, & D'Amelio, A. (2008). Resistance to change: the rest of the story.

Fundamentally, an organization with strong accountability builds trust between employer and employee, which accelerates decision-making, eases tensions between management and front-line workers, and gives people a sense that their actions, work efforts, and energies will be treated fairly.

The **B**ohn **O**rganizational **E**ngagement **S**cale [BOES] includes five questions that focus on **ACCOUNTABILITY.**

Employee Engagement and The Employee Experience do not address the element of Consequences. Here's why :

Employee engagement is focused exclusively on the individual experience of the employee, yet EE does not ask questions that address perceptions of accountability at the organizational level. This critical element of accountability is *not* assessed in employee engagement surveys.

The Employee Experience is a direct result of organizational accountability, for a company that allows shoddy work, or does not address problems in the ranks creates an environment (experience) where employees experience frustration every day.

Now that you've had an opportunity to read through and think about accountability, how would you rate your organization?

Not focused on Accountability   **Effectively managing Accountability**

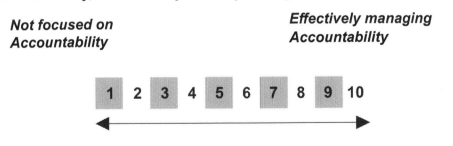

So, we've analyzed all six of the elements of Organizational Engagement.

ELEMENTS OF ORGANIZATIONAL ENGAGEMENT

1-CLARITY of Mission. Do we have confidence in where the organization is going?

2-COHESION. Can we work together to achieve mission outcomes?

3-COMMUNICATION Effectiveness. How well does the organization distribute critical information?

4-CONVICTION. Can we stay the course when times get tough?

5-Leadership COMMITMENT. Are our leaders capable of effectively achieving mission outcomes?

6-CONSEQUENCES Are people rewarded and recognized fairly?

Figure 5. The elements of OE (sample organizational results)

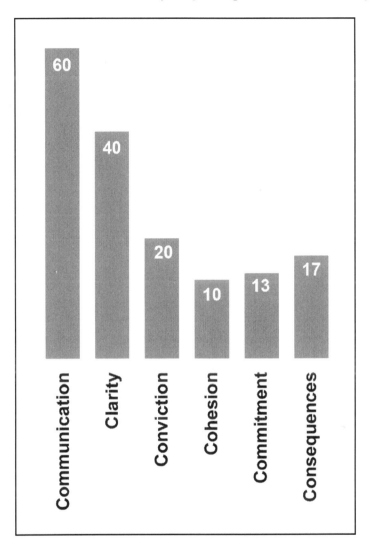

Summary of the Analysis

Figure 5 depicts the six elements of Organizational Engagement. These elements of Organizational Engagement are factors that must be managed to effect organizational transformation. Thoroughly developing a mission, improving communication, ensuring that leaders help people focus on mission, rewarding those who are achieving mission objectives through persistence and holding people accountable work together to improve organizational performance.

SECTION III — ACTION

Chapter 13

Issues that impact the six elements of
Organizational Engagement
What you need to manage

- ► Workshop findings from fifty organizational leaders revealed barriers to the six elements of Organizational Engagement: Managerial Awareness, Managerial Competence, Willingness to Solve Issues, Managerial Courage, Managerial Personality

- ► Managerial competence is the big problem.

1. **Clarity of Mission**: Do we have confidence in where the organization is going?

2. **Cohesion**: Can we work together to achieve mission outcomes?

3. **Communication Effectiveness**: How well does the organization distribute critical information?

4. **Leader Commitment**: Are our leaders capable of effectively achieving mission outcomes?

5. **Conviction/Resilience**: Can we stay the course when times get tough?

6. **Consequences/Accountability**: Are people rewarded and recognized fairly?

The things leaders must do to manage Organizational Engagement

Every element of Organizational Engagement is under the oversight of organizational leadership. Those in leadership roles have the responsibility to effectively develop, enhance and control the six elements of organizational engagement.

So, what impacts and influences the six elements of Organizational Engagement?

I wanted real-world insight into what impacts OE. So, I asked a room full of executives across a broad range of industries for their insights using a structured approach to harvesting data. Here are their insights on what it takes to manage the six elements of OE.

The process of gathering data

50+ workshop attendees gathered in groups of 5-7 people, including directors, managers, and VPs. We asked them to write down behaviors that impeded each element of organizational engagement. Hundreds of responses were evaluated and placed into categories. I am presenting the raw results. This study harvested a rich level of detail from organizational leaders who deal with organizational problems every day, and the study reveals some commonsense findings. This is a form of evidence-based practice.[132]

Developing data codes to categorize the output

The following codes naturally emerged from repeated mentions of a concept, ranging from behavior to emotion to general competence. Dropping an item into a category was a judgment call on the part of the author.

---

132 The author did not know what to expect when the data was placed into categories. What emerged is simply a result of harvesting the data, also known as Grounded Theory Approach. I discovered emerging patterns in the data. Glaser, et al.

Codes used to categorize behaviors that influence the elements of Organization Engagement[133]

MA = Managerial Awareness

Do managers know what's going on? Are managers paying attention? To employees? To customers? To issues? Or are they ignoring issues? Do they have insight into what creates and solves problems? Are they conscious of problems that must be addressed?

MC = Managerial Competence

Do managers have the capability to do things right and fix what's wrong? Are they skilled at their job of delegating, planning, and controlling? Do they have basic managerial skills? Writing skills? Technology skills?

MW = Managerial Willingness to resolve issues

Do managers have the will to change things that are not going well? Do they play the blame game? Do they kick the can down the road and ignore tough problems? Or do they persist until problems are resolved?

MCR = Managerial Courage

Are managers fearless in solving people problems? Or do they avoid conflict and do they allow poor performance to continue? Do they keep the one bad apple that is destroying the whole bunch? Do they cower in the face of struggle?

MP = Managerial Personality

How frequently does managerial personality influence Organizational Engagement? Do the aspects of emotional intelligence have an impact on the elements of OE?

---

133 All of the details from the workshop are in Appendix C. This next section is a sample of the details we harvested during the session.

To give you a sense of the work product, here is the output around Cohesion.[134]

Cohesion of workforce: What makes it difficult for people to work together?

Competing expectations	Managerial Competence
Ego / strong personalities	Managerial Personality
Lack of communication	Managerial Competence
Not having ways or tools to communicate	Managerial Competence
Workload and not given time	Managerial Competence
Leadership is subservient	Managerial Courage MCR
Lack of trust	Managerial Competence
Tolerated behavior	Managerial Courage MCR
Panic	Managerial Courage MCR
Structure	Managerial Competence
Job Threats	External
Knowledge hoarders	Managerial Willingness
Lack of time	Managerial Competence
Misaligned priorities	Managerial Competence
Personal agendas	Managerial Willingness

134 The remaining detail for the other categories is in appendix C.

Overall Results

Combining all the data from all the flipcharts and condensing it into a graph, we get the following mentions:

Managerial Competence (52 mentions] including its opposite, incompetence, stands out as the key factor influencing Organizational Engagement in every category (over 50 mentions]. Because of the number of mentions, I refine Managerial Competence a bit more in a later graph. *Thus, the day-to-day operational decisions and skills of management have the greatest impact on Organizational Engagement.*

Managerial Awareness (20 total mentions) has the greatest impact on communication and collaboration. Managers that attend to issues with teams and ensure people know what's happening are going to influence how people work together and the messages people are hearing.

Managerial Courage (17 mentions) is a major influence on the *accountability* element of OE. This is what we would expect. If managers don't have the courage to address issues, non-performers will not be held accountable and thus the organization suffers with mediocrity, bullying managers, or poor performance.

Managerial Willingness to address issues (17 total mentions) has the largest impact on *resilience*. Again, common sense would tell us that an organization populated by managers and leaders willing to press on in the face of challenges would positively influence resilience. If managers persist, followers will persist!

Managerial Personality (6 mentions) is *not* a significant influence (under 20 mentions). This is interesting because we often believe managerial personality (emotional intelligence and personality traits like narcissism have a major impact on organizations). Personality traits are inherent and notoriously difficult to change, including ego investment and narcissistic behavior, anger, bullying. This could also include elements of emotional intelligence.

Breaking the data down a bit further, we get some interesting insights.

Chart 10. What managerial behaviors influence the six elements of Organizational Engagement?

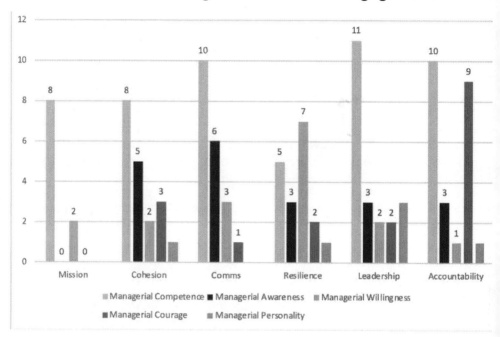

What influences Organizational Level Engagement?

Legend:
- Managerial Competence
- Managerial Awareness
- Managerial Willingness
- Managerial Courage
- Managerial Personality

Chart 10 demonstrates a fact not easily revealed by simply observing day-to-day operations. The Element of Organizational Engagement most frequently mentioned in this workshop analysis is **Accountability [24 mentions] followed by Communications [20], Leadership [19], Cohesion [19], Resilience [18] and finally, Mission [10].** Accountability has a significant impact on Organizational Engagement.

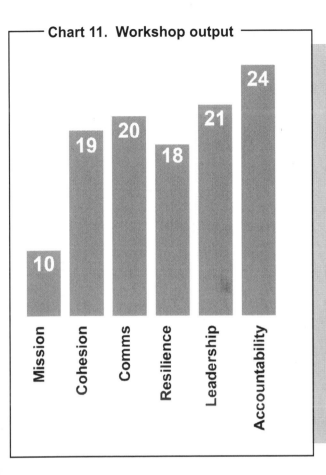

Chart 11. Workshop output

The fact that no one knew which elements would get the most mentions adds validity to the work. Any of the six elements could have stood out prominently, but Accountability was number one. Granted, the differences between accountability, comms, and leadership are not dramatic nor statistically significant (except between mission and accountability), but there is a trend.

Further calibrating the study, the specific managerial behaviors influencing the elements of organizational engagement are identified in chart 12. Strikingly, Managerial Competence is #1. (*You'll note that Managerial Courage showed up as the #1 influence on organizational accountability. Also notice Managerial Willingness showed up as #1 in resilience. These findings are what we would expect from a commonsense, nonscientific look at organizational behavior.*)

Chart 12. Managerial behaviors impacting organizational engagement

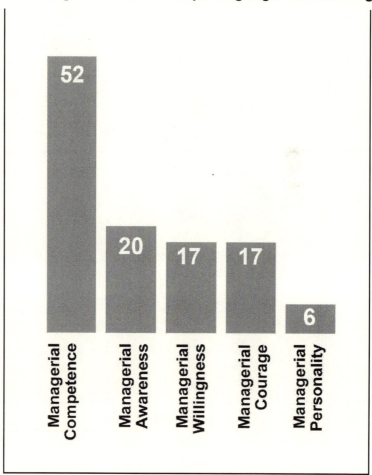

Most surprising to me is that Managerial Competence showed up so dramatically in this workshop format. We might expect things like emotional intelligence or personalities to be the biggest influencers in organizations because they are mentioned so frequently in the management literature, but *competence* showed up as #1.

Breaking this down further, I evaluated Managerial Competence by itself, because of the number of mentions. What components of Managerial Competence showed up?

Chart 13. Specific categories of Managerial Competence

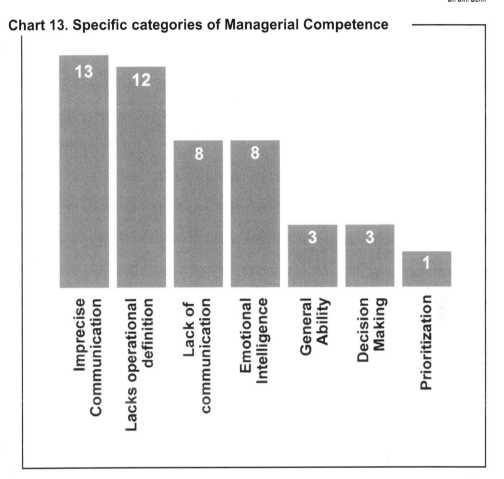

Chart 13 breaks down the Managerial Competence issues.
Imprecise communication is _**the number-one issue**_ lack operational
definitions (what is the mission? how do things work?), followed by
lack of communication. _Isn't it remarkable that "imprecise (a.k.a. lazy)
communication" tops the chart? A component of imprecise communication
is "lacks operational definition," which simply means management hasn't
taken the time to sort things out and make them workable, understandable,
and usable. Think endless PowerPoint slides without any real actionable
items, but lots of memes and charts and data that lead nowhere_ but
dominate the meetings in many organizations.

What did we learn from this data-harvesting exercise?

These specific employee and managerial behaviors have a dramatic impact on organizations, yet I wonder how much effort, focus, funding, and leadership intent is applied to these simple, even mundane, yet critical behaviors of (1) precise communication, (2) working out how things will be done operationally, and (3) ensuring general levels of communication to an organization? After all, if we want to increase levels of organizational engagement, we need to get at the roots of the problem and take corrective actions. Managerial Competence can be, well, managed!

This workshop output provides you, the reader, with a very clear set of data to analyze the effectiveness of your own organization today—right now.

Heads-up to Training and Development Teams!

The data on Managerial Competence refines where to apply effort, dollars, and training to improve Organizational Engagement. *It's time for Training and Development Teams to rethink their focus. It's time for T&D Teams to focus on Managerial Competence!*

Chapter 14

HR's role in Organizational Engagement and a Case Study

- ▶ Employee Engagement has not solved HR's dilemma
- ▶ HR needs a tool for leading organizational improvement
- ▶ OE provides HR leverage and a seat at the table, OE gives HR a playbook for implementation

"HR should become a partner with senior and line managers in strategy execution, helping to move planning from the conference room to the marketplace."[135]

This quote is from famous HR researcher Dave Ulrich—back in 1998!

Since HR has invested so heavily in Employee Engagement throughout the past two decades, the notion of using Organizational Engagement as a means for transformation raises reasonable questions about HR's role in implementing a new approach to organizational transformation.

This chapter addresses questions HR leaders posed to the author and provides the benefits to HR should they choose to use OE. It also provides a playbook for implementation. HR may feel they have a lot to lose if they invest in OE. Yes, if a company implements OE, it will lose some sunk costs, but gain much more.

---

135 Dave Ulrich, "A New Mandate for Human Resources," in *HBR* January–February 1998, p. 124.

"Off the record"

> *"I'm happy to see someone take this on because the old employee engagement models are getting stale."*

—HR Executive

Employee engagement is a beneficial tool, well known to HR, but many HR people I have spoken with off the record feel EE has seen its day and is no longer useful to organizations. Though employees have heard about EE for decades, they have seen little impact from the data, and thus are cynical about its effectiveness. As Jim Smith says, *"The real issue is nothing happens."*[136]

And employees have learned how to hack the employee engagement system. People know how to respond to surveys to get results and manipulate them to their advantage. Studies show employees don't expect their leadership to do much with the data. And the long-term global employee engagement data consistently show the same results year after year. Yet the deep, organizational performance change HR is seeking cannot happen with a workforce made cynical by an out of date tool like EE.

HR's search for a powerful tool to transform organizations

1. HR has long been in search of a strategic-level tool to create dramatic organizational improvement. The tool must be meaningful and reliable to gain the support of senior management, and it must be something that goes beyond the line level into strategic change.

2. HR has also been in search of a tool with the backing of social science research that provides concrete guidance for organizational transformation, a tool that builds a baseline of analysis and provides a clear, measurable path to deliberate action.

3. HR has been in search of a tool that includes the voices of all strata in an organization to ensure a comprehensive analysis has been conducted.

It is time for HR to exert organizational leverage.

---

136 Personal communication

OE offers a way for HR to lead the way forward.

HR has been in search of a way to execute power to change the organization. This has been an ongoing effort for some time (see the quote above from Dave Ulrich). HR wants to demonstrate their ability to influence their organization in a meaningful way. Organizational-level engagement moves away from the specific needs of individuals to mission-critical organizational change that benefits *everyone* in the long run. HR can lead the effort.

HR has seen some value from Employee Engagement, but it's time to move on.

HR representatives agree that EE has run its course, yet the hamster wheel of organizations often prevents HR from stepping toward something that can make major change. We like the status quo—it's safe. As one of my Senior HR friends told me, "No one ever got fired for suggesting the Q12 survey." Organizational Engagement gives HR an opportunity to go beyond employee engagement surveys to get employee attention. With OE, HR has a fresh method to make major operational improvement. The goals of OE are clear, the elements of what are being analyzed are precise, giving executives a clear view to how HR is working to improve the organization.

THE SIX ELEMENTS OF ORGANIZATIONAL ENGAGEMENT as identified in the Bohn Organizational Engagement Scale.

1. **Clarity of Mission**—Do we have confidence in where the organization is going?

2. **Cohesion**—Can we work together to achieve mission outcomes?

3. **Communication Effectiveness**—How well does the organization distribute critical information to everyone and provide a feedback loop?

4. **Leader Commitment**—Are our leaders capable of effectively achieving mission outcomes?

5. **Conviction / Resilience**—Can we stay the course when times get tough?

6. **Consequences/Accountability**—Are people rewarded and recognized fairly? Are resources used effectively?

OE's Value to HR

A. OE provides straightforward analysis but requires intense *long-term* focus.

Though the six elements of OE are clearly understandable, the amount of energy and leadership focus required to effectively manage each element takes serious focus. The six elements of Organizational Engagement provide HR with specific, sharply defined leverage points to improve the entire organization. They are levers meant to be used in a deliberate and strategic way after data has been acquired.

B. OE is not a check-the-box approach.

According to HR expert and consultant Greg Wilgenbusch, "Organizational Engagement analyses should *not* be conducted yearly, just to check a box." It is to be used to create organizational transformation. Measurement of OE provides a baseline to measure change and thus is a strategic resource for improvement.

C. OE provides levers to drive the culture desired by organizational leadership.

If data shows the need for improving the culture driven by communication, for instance, HR can develop a full-court communication press across the enterprise. If the culture needs to improve accountability, HR can focus there. Executives seeking to change their mission can learn where to apply the most effort. The data provided by the BOES gives HR the baseline data it has needed to make a significant transformation.[137]

D. OE is an organizational-level diagnostic tool.

Organizational-level engagement gets people thinking about the bigger picture. The current global-social and business ethos is self-focused, and people are so absorbed in their own goals, they sometimes forget they are part of something bigger. HR can apply OE for people to consider the organizational level, because the data comes from the people's perceptions of the organization!

*Employee engagement gives HR high level responses of **individual experiences** – not aggregated organizational level issues.*

---

137 OE provides metrics that are clear and manageable. Each element of Organizational Engagement stands on its own with specific questions from the survey and can be used precisely to measure change, (even to the point of T-tests if an organizational social scientist wanted to know the exact level of statistical change).

E. HR becomes the leader in development of organizational people strategy based on Organizational Engagement data.

Using organizational-level data to drive enterprise performance is the Rosetta Stone of OD. Once HR and executive leadership have a clear baseline of weaknesses and strengths, they can proceed to *work in the areas most critical for performance improvement.* Guesswork is removed. Precision is put in its place to achieve strategic change.

F. HR takes on the role it has been seeking to influence and manage deep, enduring, strategic change.

HR gets out of managing small pockets of change—departments—and exerts influence at the strategic level, providing HR the power to transform the organization using the six elements of OE. The strategic level benefits everyone. Organizational Engagement has the power to dramatically influence the enterprise in ways that cannot be achieved by EE by focusing on high-level areas for improvement.

Responding to HR's Concerns

HR people I've spoken with have raised legitimate concerns about initiating an OE program. Clearly, organizations have relied on Employee Engagement for so long, a change like this involves risk and effort. I address the objections and concerns in this next section.

Objection #1, Funding: We invested time and effort to get EE up and running.

Yes, there may be sunk costs. The opportunity for HR to leverage heavy strategic data outweighs the losses of an existing program that may only be marginally effective and is causing survey fatigue in the ranks. EE has lost momentum in making change. People are cynical and will only respond because they have to.

Objection #2, How do we explain the change to the people?

Most people are already well past employee engagement. We know it. So be clear about the rationale: "We are going to do something radically different from what we have in the past. We are looking at how all of us perceive our organization together to make deep, fundamental improvements along these six major vectors."

People will see this isn't just another survey. "We're going to examine where we have the biggest issues in the organization and we're all participating together to learn what to change. Everyone is involved." By focusing on employee autonomy in the survey, you'll increase their interest. They are getting a chance to address issues in the organization by their collective input. Explain to your organization you are committed to deep structural changes based on the input of all who participate. (*Of course, that presumes you will follow through*). Everyone from the janitor to the CEO gets their voice.

Objection #3, The current process is in place, and we know what to do.

Yes, it takes effort to change, but if EE isn't changing the organization, will additional effort make things better in the long run? *Does escalated commitment to anything make a failing cause better?* It's best to think of this as you would technology: it's no different than improving technology that increases performance. The value of learning organizational weaknesses and managing organizational-level transformation overshadows the effort required to put OE in place.

What advantages does HR gain by implementing OE?

ADVANTAGE #1 - Survey anonymity

One of the greatest HR advantages is this: **survey anonymity**. When people participate in OE, they are reflecting the *organization*, not their individual concerns. Fear that controversial opinions will be reveaeld is a concernfor many people taking surveys. Assessing at the organizational level takes the pressure off the individual and puts it on the organization. *OE gives people a new way to analyze their organizations without fear of reprisal.*

ADVANTAGE #2 – Reboot the system

Fresh organizational learning gives the company **a chance to reboot**. You are literally overcoming sludge in the system by moving from a tool with a longstanding organizational familiarity to something fresh.

ADVANTAGE #3 HR is driving the people side of the business!

By gaining organizational engagement data, HR can lead organizational improvement in very specific ways:

1. **Finding the weakest link:** Analyzing Organizational Engagement at the departmental level allows organizations to discover and strengthen their weakest link, enhancing the performance of the entire organization, by taking the high-level analysis, focusing sharply, then looking at disparities at geographic or other logical locations.

2. **Prioritizing to spend training dollars wisely:** Organizational Engagement data analysis directs an organization where to focus budget, managerial effort, and training to improve performance. Data will show one of the six vectors to be mission critical and worthy of top priority.

3. **Planning for success prior to change**: The **B**ohn **O**rganizational **E**ngagement **S**cale assesses how teams and organizations will manage new challenges. Deficits can be addressed to ensure the team has a greater likelihood of success during significant organizational change.

4. **Analyzing exemplar teams and groups** to assess why they have such a strong level of performance. Leverage that knowledge to improve an entire organization. Organizations that take the time to invest in a study of organizational engagement find the best leaders who can teach others. Take a high-level analysis and then focus sharply, looking at geographic disparities.

5. **Change management** requires an organization that is focused and has the capacity and leadership to achieve change outcomes. Is the organization ready? OE can assess the capabilities of teams, divisions, and entire enterprises by detecting weak spots in the organization.

6. **Activating new strategies** requires an organization that can generate maximum people involvement. Is the organization capable of moving forward?

7. **Removing bad actors** is far more effective when an organization can sort out teams or departments who are damaging organizational-level engagement.

8. **Ceasing escalated commitment:** Get rid of the projects that are depleting resources and sapping the precious resource of human motivation.

   These are organizational-level impacts HR can lead. But they cannot be addressed until a corporation assesses itself at the enterprise level. *Once an OE analysis has been done, the organization can move forward.*

A Case Study: ACME Industries

- ► **Case study in Organizational Engagement**
- ► **Observations and learning**

For HR and Operations

I added this case study to demonstrate the impact of assessing Organizational Level Engagement using the **B**ohn **O**rganizational **E**ngagement **S**cale (**BOES**). Though the organization's identity has been removed, this case study shows the impact of evaluating engagement at the organizational level.

ACME Organization

ACME is a multinational corporation with operations in Europe, North America, and Asia. Management recognized that employees were critical to their successful growth. They launched a human capital development initiative to build an engaged staff that is productive, motivated and committed to the long-term success of the business. The first phase of this initiative was the deployment of a company-wide assessment using the **B**ohn **O**rganizational **E**ngagement **S**cale **(BOES)** for the purpose of defining the initiatives to help improve the workforce's engagement, motivation, and loyalty.

Highlights of the evaluation

This is ACME's baseline that serves to measure improvement. Over 400 respondents participated from multiple locations across the world. Strong participation rates are an indicator of employee interest in the survey process (low participation indicates low interest). Overall/global participation rates for ACME were strong at 74.6%. Plant location participation rates varied. ACME's Global OE scores, shown below, have much room for improvement. Taking the effort to assess an organizational baseline provided ACME data to build upon. Questions were provided both at the corporate and local leadership level.

The BOES measures all six elements using 30 items, as articulated above.

6 = the highest score possible, while 1 = lowest score.

Categories of Organizational Engagement

Chart 13. Engagement by factor (Global Questions only)

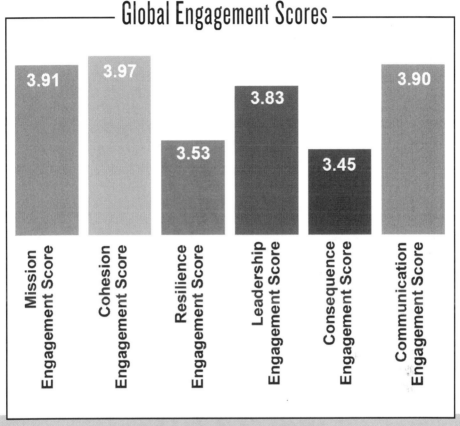

Global Engagement Scores

3.91	3.97	3.53	3.83	3.45	3.90
Mission Engagement Score	Cohesion Engagement Score	Resilience Engagement Score	Leadership Engagement Score	Consequence Engagement Score	Communication Engagement Score

6=top score; 1=lowest score

Clarity of Mission: Are we confident in where the organization is going?

Cohesion: Can we work together to achieve mission outcomes?

Communication Effectiveness: How well does the organization distribute critical information?

Resilience: Can we stay the course when times get tough? (Lower score is better)

Leader Commitment: Are our leaders capable of effectively achieving mission outcomes?

Consequences/Accountability Are people rewarded and recognized fairly?

The results

Results varied across geographies, but overall, ACME team members had a sense the organization was working together reasonably well at the global level, yet with much room for improvement. Recall that a 6 is the highest score for any of these factors. **The global Cohesion score of 3.97 out of 6.00**

Different departments; different responses

HR, finance, and sales groups tended to rank questions higher overall compared to operations and engineering team members. ACME leadership had an opportunity to develop conversations between these groups to gain an understanding of why they see things so differently and thus improve organizational perspective on how the company is doing. Operations and engineering, as in most organizations, tend to have lower scores across the survey.

Thus, the BOES was valuable in demonstrating demographic and geographic differences across the six elements of OE. Geographically dispersed groups did not feel connected into the broader corporation and sensed that the global organization could work together more effectively. The various office locations believed the global organization could be more effective in sharing operational knowledge and connecting people together.

ACME Consequence Engagement Scores

Consequence engagement scores were consistently low across most locations and organizational groups on a global and local engagement basis. Specific areas that needed to be addressed included fairness of promotions, rewards, and accountability. Management personnel changes were under analysis after the data was presented to executive leadership.

ACME Resilience Scores

High scores regarding the ability to adequately address an economic downturn and create strong, long-term growth *have created a higher than desired* resilience engagement score. (Resilience questions are negatively worded and thus should be low. For example: "I doubt this company will be here in 5 years.") Strategic direction needed to be carefully thought through and distributed to the field to ensure team members had a clear view of how the strategy would help the organization weather economic storms and develop a sense of future accomplishments to increase momentum.

ACME Corporate Leadership scores—Good news for global leadership team

The data showed a general sense that Global Leadership knew where they were going **(GLOBAL LEADERSHIP SCORE 3.83).** This was something to build on. People trusted that their corporate leadership had the capability to move the organization forward. The corporate leadership questions generally had higher scores, irrespective of location. That is good news. ACME needed to carefully articulate where it was going and how it intended to get there.

The value?

Armed with OE data and information, this organization was set to make specific, *foundational changes* around the six elements of OE.

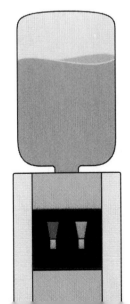

Chapter 15

Conclusion and Recommendations

▶ **Organizational Engagement is the level of motivation activated by employee perceptions of their organization's ability to achieve outcomes.**

Organizational Engagement focuses on six elements of organizational behavior required to enhance organizational performance. As we have seen, analyzing Organizational Engagement gets to the root of organizational ineffectiveness and builds employee confidence in an organization's ability to achieve outcomes.

The Six Elements of Organizational Engagement

1. **Clarity of Mission**: Do we have confidence in where the organization is going?

2. **Cohesion**: Can we work together to achieve mission outcomes?

3. **Communication Effectiveness**: How well does the organization distribute critical information?

4. **Leadership Commitment**: Are our leaders capable of effectively achieving mission outcomes?

5. **Resilience and Conviction**: Can we stay the course when times get tough?

6. **Consequences/Accountability:** Are people rewarded and recognized fairly?

Let's revisit the organizational distresses. I offer some practical action for each, based on OE.

Chart 14. Organizational Distress and OE Considerations

Business Distress	Missing Element of Organizational Engagement
O.A.D.D., Organizational Attention Deficit Disorder	Lack of **Mission** Focus
Recognition Anorexia	**Leadership** issue
Organizational Co-dependency	**Leadership** issue
Organizational Narcissism	**Accountability** issue
Anxiety leading to panic attacks	This can be a combination of **Communication**, **Leadership** and lack of **Mission** focus.
Organizational Depression	A lack of **Mission** focus, a lack of **Leadership** success, and uncertainty (poor **Communication**).

Recall the organizational distresses described in Chapter 3. *Things that happen at the organizational level require organizational-level correction.* One or more of the Six elements of Organizational-Level Engagement reveals the root issue of these distresses. Diagnosing which elements are the causes of organizational distress will enable leaders to select the appropriate corrective action required to improve these organizational conditions.

Summing it up

Let's take one last look at all the elements of OE and consider their impact on organizational performance.

The elements influence the outcomes

Each element of Organizational Engagement influences organizational outcomes. Mission impacts revenue, and an ill-chosen mission will result in financial ruin. Cohesion influences ROI because effectiveness speeds financial returns. Communication influences turnover, absenteeism and productivity, leader commitment influences everything! Conviction influences Profit and Revenue and consequences influence turnover and absenteeism.

Figure 6. OE and organizational performance.

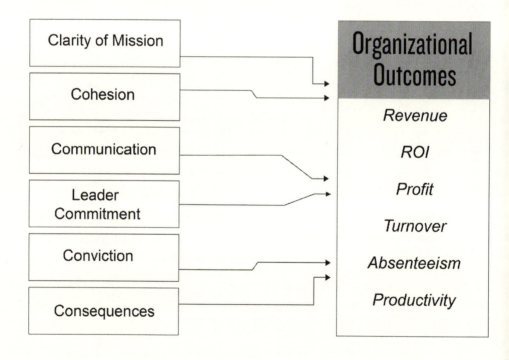

Consider the financial impact of Organizational Engagement.

Finally, and critically, we return to the beginning: The purpose of measuring and managing Organizational Engagement is to ensure the success of the organization. Recall that organizational performance—financial outcomes, market share, profitability, revenue, customer satisfaction, and quality—happens at a high level when all the elements of the organization are functioning effectively together at a high level.

The financial indicators discussed earlier are shown in Chart 15. These metrics are universal for all companies worldwide. Each element of Organizational Engagement influences these metrics, some more than others. *Thus, we see that the elements of OE are not soft skills.* They make or break the organization.

Chart 15. Matrix, The Impact of Organizational Engagement on Financial Metrics[138]

Factors that drive financial results	Clarity of Mission	Cohesion	Conviction / Resilience	Leadership Commitment	Communication	Consequences
ROI Budgets met						
Opportunity Costs						
Productivity / Turnover						
Process costs / waste / Inefficiency / Cycle time						
Growth and Revenues						
Innovation						
Leverage and Scale (2+2=5)						

---

138 Chart courtesy of Lisa Howard.

Employee Engagement does not solve these issues!

Although there are correlation studies that demonstrate relationships between financials and employee engagement (yes, they do exist), employee engagement does not focus on these elements of financial impact. Employees are always concerned about their immediate needs. Ultimately, they'll want to work at (and *stay with*!) an organization that is firing on all cylinders. They'll work hard for a company that displays a clear mission, employs people who work well together, communicates effectively, has leadership that gets the job done, knows how to stay the course, holds people accountable for their work—and makes a profit.

People love a winner — and financial outcomes predict winners.

Organizational Achievements require organizational-level actions.

We end where we began. Organizational outcomes are a result of effective organizational inputs. Employees can assess the six elements of organizational engagement, and those perceptions influence the amount of motivation they exert for the organization. Organizational performance is the outcome of all six elements of organization engagement functioning at profound levels. Organizational engagement is critical to organizational success.

In summary:

If an organization consistently treats people with fairness based on work quality

If an organization has leaders who get things done ... and

If an organization can persist in the face of obstacles,

If an organization consistently shares important information with all members,

If an organization has people who work together effectively,

If an organization has a clear view of what is ahead,

It will have a high level of Organizational Engagement.

Figure 7. The six elements

Clarity of Mission
Do we know where we're going?

Consequences
Are people held
accountable for
their actions?

Cohesion
Can we work
together?

Communication
How effective are
our communication
processes?

Leader Commitment
How effective are our
leaders at getting
things done?

Conviction
Can we stay the
course when things
get tough?

Taken together, these six elements of organizational engagement impact how your company will perform against competition in the marketplace, how it will retain employees, how it will generate new ideas, how it will increase profitability, and how it will build its reputation. .

People in your company are talking about the six elements of Organizational Engagement at your water cooler right now.

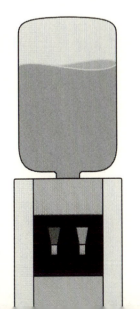

What are people saying about your organization?

SECTION IV— APPENDICES

Snapshot Analysis: What you can do _today!_

Six Elements of Organizational Engagement

1. Organizational Mission Focus

   a. How clear is your mission?

   b. How far down into the organization does your mission reach? How do you know?

   c. How would people define the mission of your organization?

Organizational Simplification

- Get rid of excessive (and often unnecessary) policies

- Take inventory of programs

- Removing old corporate policies is like cleaning your garage: you don't want to, but the world is a better place when it's done.

- Old strategies = organizational sediment

- Excessive policies become organizational sludge

- Simplify your organization every day. Organizations attract complexity. Reduce complexity; improve performance.

2. Organizational Level Collaboration

a. What processes do you have to build in collaboration as part of daily operations?

b. How are your leaders rewarded for collaboration?

o Between team members

o Between departments

o Between divisions

o Between geographies

3. Organizational Level Communication

a. What is your feedback loop?

b. How are leaders rewarded for communication?

c. How do you *know* communication is reaching all levels?

4. Organizational Conviction, Resilience

a. Who are your exemplars of persistence within the ranks? Publish those examples.

b. Does your senior leadership conduct seminars where people hear stories of persistence in the face of trouble?

c. What do people fear in your ranks?

5. Leadership Skill Development

a. How are your leaders evaluated against the six elements of organizational engagement?

b. How are your leaders rewarded for getting the job done?

c. How are leaders trained to bring about collective achievements?

6. Organizational Accountability—

Consequences

a. Evaluate Organizational Reward systems

b. Look for examples of unfair treatment in the form of promotions, perks, or pay

c. Evaluate employee performance systems

   o How do you ensure clarity in expectations and reward appropriately?

   o How do you provide organizational training in effective recognition practices?

   o When was the last time you evaluated the fairness of promotional processes?

   o Do you have the courage to assess the relevance of breathing dinosaur projects (and the additional courage to STOP them in their tracks)?

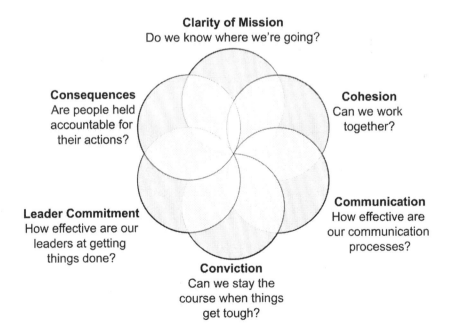

Clarity of Mission
Do we know where we're going?

Consequences
Are people held
accountable for
their actions?

Cohesion
Can we work
together?

Communication
How effective are
our communication
processes?

Leader Commitment
How effective are our
leaders at getting
things done?

Conviction
Can we stay the
course when things
get tough?

Appendix B

Methods of Organizational Analysis (from p. 45)

I. Organizational Culture

Culture: exactly what is it?

One of the major challenges in organizational analysis is the definition of "culture." It is an oblique word with as many meanings as there are people in the room. Culture is a glamorous, intriguing word and it has the sophisticated ring of … well, *culture!* The problem is, culture is often vague and difficult to pin down (and thus difficult to operationalize and change). Deference to culture allows those who do not want to change the ability to say, "it's a cultural issue," providing them an excuse to continue on with their same old practices.

Culture is "the glue that binds an organization together … it is the collection of values, beliefs, symbols, and norms the organization follows and that define what it is and how it does business each and every day" (SHRM, Fornal, 2002). Ask anyone in your organization to define culture, and you'll get as many definitions as there are people.

Cultural analyses, while helpful, still do not provide specific solutions to the problems of the culture itself. Let me explain. Foundational researchers would offer that "culture is the way we do things around here." If that's the case, and we want to improve the way we do things, we need to resolve what it is we're doing, what we're doing and *how those actions influence outcomes.* After that, we can make changes that correct the way we do things. If culture is 'the way we do things around here," why not analyze that? Ineffective organizational culture costs thousands, even millions, for organizations every year.

Important for our analysis is this: Albert Bandura wrote, "Because of their diverse impact, *an organization's beliefs about its engagement to produce results* is undoubtedly an important feature of its operative culture." (italics mine)[139] In short, what people believe about their aggregate capability to perform is crucial to long-term organizational success.

---

139 Bandura, A. (1997). *Self-efficacy: The exercise of control.* New York: W. H. Freeman. (Italics mine)

The truth is: *Culture* cannot effectively be analyzed at the individual level. Employee engagement says very little about "how things are done around here." It is too focused on the individual employee to analyze such a high, strategic level of enterprise behavior.

II. OCAI Instrument

The OCAI (Organizational Culture Assessment Instrument[140]) emphasizes culture types within different organizations, including Dominant Archetypes of Clan Culture, Adhocracy Culture, Market Culture, and Hierarchy Culture (essentially different ways of working and approaching the world outside). This is a prominent instrument in organizational assessment (one of the top fifty in the world, I am told). The approach assesses the framework of organizational culture, in other words, *the way we do things around here.* In some ways, the OCAI addresses the inevitable evolution of organizations from adhocracy to hierarchy. One of the difficulties of using this instrument is that it doesn't get at specific behavioral level actions organizations need to change to improve.

III. Organization-Based Self-Esteem

This measurement is focused on how an individual feels about himself or herself within an organization. In other words, how does participation in a specific organization contribute to one's self-esteem?[141]

Quinn and Cameron state:

"The evidence from our review of more than four dozen empirical studies supports the claim that an individual's self-esteem, formed around work and organizational experiences, as reflected by *organization-based self-esteem* (italics mine), may well play a significant role in shaping employee intrinsic motivation, work-related attitudes (e.g., turnover intentions, job satisfaction, organizational commitment) and behaviors (e.g., performance, citizenship behavior, turnover)."

In addition, the evidence supports the claim that work environment structures that provide opportunities for the exercise of *self*-direction and *self*-control may promote organization-based *self*-esteem. When employees are told that they "make a difference around here," and that those

---

140 Robert E. Quinn, Kim S. Cameron, *Diagnosing and Changing Organizational Culture: Based on the Competing Values Framework*, Third Edition: Jossey-Bass, 2011.

141 Pierce, Jon & Gardner, Donald & L. Cummings, L & Dunham, Randall. (1989). "Organization-based self-esteem: Construct definition, measurement, and validation." *Academy of Management Journal.* 32. 622-48.

differences are valued by the organization, it impacts their self-concept. Organization-based opportunities for positive and successful experiences were also found to have a positive relationship with OBSE.

This organizational analysis is focused on how the individual responds to the way that the organization supports an emotional response, not the organization's ability to produce output. *It is the individual's view of the organization.*

IV. Organizational Commitment

Organizational commitment has been conceptualized as *"an individual's attitude towards the organization*, consisting of a strong belief in, and acceptance of, an organization's goals, willingness to exert considerable effort on behalf of the organization and a strong desire to maintain membership in the organization."[142]

It was noted in their study that affective commitment to the organization resulted in low turnover and lower absenteeism. *The individual's view of the organization is still the lens is also used in this approach. What is the organization doing for me so I may do something to benefit it?*

V. Organizational Climate

Kopelman, Brief and Guzzo wrote, "Climate is the psychological process that mediates the relationships between the work environment (conceived as an objective set of organizational policies, practices, and procedures) and work-related attitudes and behaviors."[143] Climate includes the following five things: *autonomy, reward, support, participation, and warmth.* This is sometimes referred to as "psychological climate." One primary aspect of climate is "socioemotional support," which is *"the extent to which employees perceive* that their personal welfare is protected by kind, considerate, and generally humane management."

Again, the individual's view of self within the organization is the lens used by this approach. Does the person feel cared for in the context of this organization?

---

142 Eby, Lillian & M. Freeman, Deena & C. Rush, Michael & Lance, Chuck. (1999). "Motivational bases of affective organizational commitment: A partial test of an integrative theoretical model." *Journal of Occupational and Organizational Psychology.* 72. 463–83. (italics mine)

143 Kopelman, Richard; Brief, Arthur; & Guzzo, R.A.. (1990). "The role of climate and culture in productivity." *Organizational climate and culture.* 282-318., 295.

VI.   Organizational Citizenship

The construct of organizational citizenship has also been measured at the group level.[144] Organizational citizenship behaviors include such things as "helping others with their jobs, volunteering for additional work, and supporting organizational objectives."[145] The purpose for measuring this construct is to assess how much additional effort people are willing to expend in pursuit of organizational objectives. Productivity and performance are the primary goals of such instruments and interventions.[146]

What inspires organizational citizenship? How is it that people feel so much a part of an organization that they are willing to expend additional effort? **Organizational Health**

Patrick Lencioni's book, *The Advantage* (2012) touts Organizational Health as a means to improving enterprise effectiveness. While it is a significant accomplishment, it focuses primarily on the leadership team and clarity of mission. Its value is that it looks at the enterprise—the organization. Yet, it does not ask how the organization functions as a whole. Lencioni's premise is that *leadership teams* can only be effective if they are cohesive (acting in one supportive accord with each other), and he bases cohesion on the five dysfunctions: He illustrates this in pyramid form from bottom to top: "Trust and Respect, Conflict, Accountability, Commitment, Delivering Results." An overall view of how the organization functions is still not part of the analysis.

VII.   Maybe the secret lies in Six Sigma and Lean

For Organizational Transformation to take place, we need specifics. Let's do process mapping, Lean Sigma, let's build scores of projects that increase ROI. *Yet we know the project approach does not solve questions at the organizational level.* While we may increase the number of cost saving projects, we still do not understand the bigger issues of why an organization at large remains ineffective.

VIII.   Perceived Organizational Support

Eisenberger gets a little closer to an organizational focus. "Management must be constantly on guard to be sure that the bureaucracy of the organization facilitates the basic goals and objectives of the organization rather than interfering with them."[147] But he is still focused

---

144   Organ, 1990.
145   Judge et al., 2001, p. 381, citing Borman & Motowidlo, 1993, and Organ, 1990.
146   See also Lee, K., & Allen, N. J. (2002).
147   P.83

on the individual. Perceived Organizational Support is about how the organization supports the individual, not the other way around. *Again, it is the individual's view of how the organization provides support.*

IX.   Balanced Scorecard?

Norton and Kaplan developed a rather famous piece of work entitled *The Balanced Scorecard*, which is still highly regarded and used in organizations. They cite four elements of organizational performance: [148]

Financial: Often renamed stewardship or something else,, this perspective views organizational financial performance and the use of financial resources.

Customer/ Stakeholder: This perspective views organizational performance from the point of view the customer or other key stakeholders that the organization is designed to serve.

Internal Process: Views organizational performance through the lenses of the quality and efficiency related to product or services or other key business processes.

Organizational Capacity (originally called Learning and Growth): views organizational performance through the lenses of human capital, infrastructure, technology, culture and other capacities that are key to breakthrough performance.

These four lenses of organizational effectiveness are useful analytical tools to be sure, yet even this significantly powerful framework does not address some key questions: What makes an organization tick? And what should we do to improve it?

X.   Employee Engagement

Fostered by Buckingham and Coffman's *Break All the Rules* and Gallup's Q12, employee engagement remains a key focus among organizations. Employee Engagement is the *individual's view of their situation* within the organization.

---

148 Kaplan and Norton, "Using the balanced scorecard as a strategic management system." *HBR*, Jan–Feb1996, 76.

Appendix C

Workshop harvesting
Workshop output

Analyzing each element of Organizational Engagement by number of mentions.

MA – Managerial awareness MW – Managerial willingness MP – Managerial Personalities	MC – Managerial competence MCR – Managerial courage
Clarity of Mission: Why are people uncertain about direction?	
Lack of communication of direction	MC
Executive team not aligned	MW
Owners background	MP
Not defined in real speak	MC
Not actionable or attainable	MC
Reactive	MC
Not defined	MC
Marketplace uncertainty	External
Not easy	MC
Skills gap	MC
Disney statement	MC
Accountability	MW

MA – Managerial awareness MW – Managerial willingness MP – Managerial Personalities	MC – Managerial competence MCR – Managerial courage
Cohesion of workforce: What makes it difficult for people to work together?	
Competing expectations	MC
Ego – strong personalities	MP
Lack of communication	MC
Not having 'ways' or 'tools' to communicate	MC
Workload and not given time	MC
Leadership is subservient	MCR
Lack of trust	MC
Tolerated behavior	MCR
Panic	MCR
Structure	MC
Job Threats	External
Knowledge hoarders	MW
Lack of time	MC
Misaligned priorities	MC
Personal agendas	MW

MA – Managerial awareness MW – Managerial willingness MP – Managerial Personalities	MC – Managerial competence MCR – Managerial courage
Communications between members of workforce: **How do we share information?**	
Too busy	MC
Not enough follow-up and 'done'	MC
Too many buzzwords	MC
Not explaining context	MC
How it affects them	MA
Relevance	MC
Agenda unclear	MC
Wrong type of communication (written vs. verbal)	MC
Lack of listening	MA
Lack of 2-way communication	MC
Don't know audience	MA
Not prioritized	MW
Too busy	MW
Lack of focus	MW
Lack context	MA
Methods	MC
Say one thing, mean another	MCR
Generational disconnect	MA
Same old information	MC
Lack of relevance	MA

MA – Managerial awareness MW – Managerial willingness MP – Managerial Personalities	MC – Managerial competence MCR – Managerial courage

Conviction to persist: What limits resilience?	
Change of management	MW
Flavor change	MW
Blah blah blah (useless words)	MW
Tone of management – panic or calm	MCR
Can we keep pace with change or evolution?	MCR
Inflexible processes	MW
Lack of staff involvement	MA
Inability to address root cause	MW
Unclear direction	MC
Past failures	MA
Poor leadership	
▶ Won't change	MW
▶ Bad communicator	MC
▶ Decision making	MC
▶ Trust	MP
▶ Lack of Recognition	MW
Succession planning	MC
Burn out	MA
Transparency to problem	MA
Lack of innovation	MW
Content	MC

MA – Managerial awareness MW – Managerial willingness MP – Managerial Personalities	MC – Managerial competence MCR – Managerial courage

Leader Commitment – What accounts for poor leadership?	
Frequent leadership changes	MC
Lack of alignment	MW
Personal agendas	MP
Lack of measures metrics/ (emotion-based decisions)	MC
Not understanding real world	MA
Shiny object	MC
No clear plan or strategy	MC
Tell/Say vs. Do/Action	MA
Inconsistent messaging	MC
Lack of follow-up and support	MC
Poor delegation	MC
Not a team player	MW
Lack of direction	MC
Improper training not enough experience	MC
Too many chiefs	MP
No ownership	MC
Lack of flexibility	MA
Throwing weight around	MP
Lack of respect (employees don't respect)	MA
Lack of accountability	MCR
Undermining decisions	MCR
Micromanagement	MC

MA – Managerial awareness MW – Managerial willingness MP – Managerial Personalities	MC – Managerial competence MCR – Managerial courage

Consequences and Accountability:
Why don't organizations hold people accountable?

Fear of conflict	MCR
Avoidance of issues	MCR
Lower Expectations	MCR
Loss of Tribal Knowledge – (Fear)	MCR
Inconsistency in policies and Lack of policies	MC
Goals – Training – Accountability	MC
Rewarding Fire Fighting	MC
No clarity – mission/vision	MC
No expectations or follow-up	MC
Scope is too broad	MC
No metrics/measures	MC
Lack of transparency	MP
Want/expect 2nd chances	MCR
Lack of clarity – top down	MC
Competing metrics	MA
Too many things to accomplish at once	MA
Frequent changes in direction	MC
Changes in organizational structure – new managers	MC
Lack of trickle down from management	MA
Managers don't take the time	MW
Lack of candidates	external
Allowing legacies and favoritism	MCR
Perception of legal limitations	MCR
Workload not distributed fairly	MCR
Different departments not held to same standards	MCR

Appendix D

Albert Bandura's Efficacy theory[149] in the context of Organizations Social science support for Organizational Engagement.

Bandura's Theory of Efficacy	What events, symbols or behaviors in an organization turn this aspect of the theory into action?
Enactive Mastery (Performance Accomplishments) "Look at what we did."	✔ Completion of projects ✔ Inventions ✔ Awards ✔ Publications ✔ Performance Reports ✔ Sales accomplishments (being awarded a large contract) ✔ Effective Reengineering projects ✔ Sales Performance ✔ History of the company ✔ Acquisition of other businesses
Vicarious Modeling "If Jenny can do this, so can I" "If Customer Service can do this, so can we."	✔ Promotions ✔ Completion of degree programs ✔ Departmental performance ✔ Capability of my department ✔ Capability of my manager ✔ Coworkers who accomplish great things
Verbal Persuasion "You can do it"	✔ Speeches at all levels ✔ Staff meetings ✔ Daily communication with staff ✔ Encouragement from coworkers ✔ Written communication
Physiological Arousal "The fear factor"	✔ Downsizing (-) ✔ Restructuring (-) ✔ Recognition Events (+) ✔ Funding (+) ✔ Resources (+) ✔ Lack of resources (-) ✔ Negative Managerial behavior (-) ✔ Change (-)

---

149 Bandura, A. (1997). *Self-efficacy: The exercise of control.* New York: W. H. Freeman.

A review of the distresses along with detailed analyses for improvement

I. O.A.D.D. Organizational Attention Deficit Disorder

OADD is like schizophrenia which comes from *schizein* and *phren*, two Greek words meaning, literally, a split mind. Organizational uncertainty, team infighting, ineffective and diluted distribution of resources are symptoms of this distress.

Treatment: Focus on Mission and Clarity

1. Leadership must refocus the organization!

2. Choose the critical few initiatives from the agreed upon strategy, and say "no" to the rest.

3. Get rid of breathing dinosaurs (projects with no future).

4. Be deliberate about where to focus energy and stay the course.

5. Discover the disconnect. Who is uncommitted to the organizational direction? Why?

6. If there is a high-level team member who is traveling in a direction that diminishes the effectiveness of the organization, remove them.

II. Recognition Anorexia

Organizations talk about recognition, but they do very little because they're worried "people will slow down or stop working because we gave them recognition." The social science data shows that not to be true.

Treatment: Focus on leadership and accountability

1. Organizational and individual achievements must be celebrated and heralded across the organization.
2. Improve the quality of performance reviews.
3. Understand that achievements are a source of engagement and that they build strength for the next challenge.

III. Organizational Co-Dependency

In organizations with co-dependency, consultants have become a crutch, using the consultant as a facilitator for understanding all the problems within our company, yet rarely if ever resolving them. In some cases, consultants manage whole parts of the business.

Treatment: Focus on Leadership

1. Ask whether the consultant has truly helped your organization over the long haul. If not, fire the consultant.

2. Better still, build in a portion of their fee to withhold if things go poorly.

3. And, if you still need them, build transfer of their expertise to your staeff into the contract.

IV. Organizational Narcissism, a.k.a hubris

Business is losing ground, but executives are *so proud of their past achievements* that they cannot see how fast the future is hurtling toward them. This is especially true of self-made entrepreneurs who have been wildly successful for decades but have lost sight of what is happening around them as the business grows out of control.

Treatment: Focus on Leadership and Accountability

1. Listen to front-line people and customers!
2. Conduct an honest assessment of the current state of the organization and its place in the market.
3. Intentionally hire people from the outside to bring in fresh ideas and (effectively) shake things up.
4. Remind people that many companies who once were thought to be Titans went down in flames because of hubris.

V. Organizational Anxiety leading to panic attacks

When Anxiety Disorder takes hold, you look around your organization and notice people are unable to think clearly. They demonstrate frustration with each other and are sensitive to things that would normally not be an issue. They overreact or are paralyzed and unable to make decisions.

Treatment: Focus on Leadership, Communication, and Resilience

1. Find the things that can be controlled and manage them quickly, including communication about what is being done (to reduce immediate anxiety).
2. Hire temporary members and staff up as needed and have managers/leaders step in to fill orders to get through the crisis.
3. If the problem is a failed organizational initiative, stop it dead in its tracks. Sunk costs notwithstanding, some projects simply are not worth the additional escalated commitment. No need to persist in a failed mission.
4. In the case of a failed product or safety mishap, get the help of an expert PR person and follow their advice.

VI. Organizational Depression

People are listless and not generating new ideas. They are engaged in social loafing and complaining more than in getting the work done. The sources of Organizational Depression vary, but the most likely issue is one of inconsistent direction causing people to feel like their time and effort is wasted. They mark time and fold their arms waiting for something significant to redirect the organization.

Treatment: Focus on Mission, Communication, and Leadership

1. HR cannot just check the boxes! Do an honest appraisal of consistent employee feedback and investigate other organizational data.
2. If there's an ineffective manager or leader with a track record of employee complaints, get them to move on. Your people will thank you.
3. Find an enlightened leader who can change the culture to one of gratitude.
4. Ensure the recognition is earned, and, if it has been, reward appropriately.

References

Anderson, E. (2012, January 18). "Why top talent leaves: Top 10 reasons boiled down to 1." *Forbes* blog. https://www.forbes.com/sites/erikaandersen/2012/01/18/why-top-talent-leaves-top-10-reasons-boiled-down-to-1/#5c21b9204e43

Ng,K., Ang, S., & Chan, K. (2008) Personality and leader effectiveness: a moderated mediation model of leadership self-efficacy, job demands, and job autonomy. Journal of Applied Psychology 2008, 93 (4): 733-43

Aon Hewitt (2016). *2016 Trends in global employee engagement: Employee engagement is on the rise, but volatility abounds*. Deerfield, IL: Author.

Armenakis, A., Harris, S., Cole, M., Fillmer, L., & Self, D. (2008). "A top management team's reaction to organizational transformation: The diagnostic benefits of five key change sentiments." *Journal of Change Management, 7*(3), 273-290.

Bandura. A. (1986). *Social foundations of thought and action*. Englewood Cliffs: Prentice Hall.

Bandura, A. (1993). "Perceived self-efficacy in cognitive development and functioning." *Educational Psychologist, 28*(2), 117-148.

Bandura, A. (1997). *Self-efficacy: The exercise of control*. New York: W. H. Freeman.

Bareil, C., Savoie, A, & Meunier, S. (2007). "Patterns of discomfort with organizational change." *Journal of Change Management, 7*(1), 13-24.

Barends, A. (2016). *Global Employee Engagement Index* (vol. 3). Amsterdam: Effectory International.

Barling, J., & Beattie, R. (1983). "Self-efficacy beliefs and sales performance." *Journal of Organizational Behavior Management 5*(1), 41-51.

Becker, W., & Cropanzano, R. (2010). Organizational neuroscience: The promise and prospects of an emerging discipline. *Journal of Organizational Behavior, 31*(7), 1055-1059.

Bennis, W. G. (1989). *On becoming a leader*. Reading, MA: Addison-Wesley.

Bennis. W. G., & Nanus, B. (1985). *Leaders: The strategies for taking charge*. New York: Harper & Row.

Bohn, J. G. (2001). *The design and development of an instrument to assess organizational efficacy.* (Unpublished doctoral dissertation.) University of Wisconsin–Milwaukee.

Bohn, J. G. (2010). "Development and exploratory validation of an organizational engagement scale." *Human Resource Development Quarterly, 21*(3), 227-251.

Bolman, L., & Deal, T. (1992) "What makes a team work?" *Organizational Dynamics, 21*(2), 34-44.

Borman, W. C., & Motowidlo, S. M. (1993). "Expanding the criterion domain to include elements of contextual performance." In N. Schmitt & W. C. Borman (Eds.), *Personnel Selection in Organizations* (pp. 71-98). San Francisco: Jossey-Bass.

Brandt, G. (2013, September 18). "When employee engagement becomes counterproductive." *Forbes* blog. Retrieved from https://www.forbes.com/sites/georgebradt/2013/09/18/when-employee-engagement-becomes-counterproductive/#24fa85272911

Brett, J. F., & Luciano, M. M. (2018, October 18). 3 steps for engaging health care providers in organizational change. *Harvard Business Review.* Retrieved from https://hbr.org/2018/10/3-steps-for-engaging-health-care-providers-in-organizational-change

Bruch, H., & Ghoshal, S. (2003). "Unleashing organizational energy." *MIT Sloan Management Review, 45*(1), 45-51.

Buckingham, M., & Coffman, C. (1999). *First, break all the rules: What the world's greatest managers do differently.* New York, NY: Simon & Schuster.

Burke, M. (2018). "What are the top issues facing HR executives? Our predictions for 2019. Aon blog." Retrieved from https://insights.humancapital.aon.com/talent-rewards-and-performance/what-are-the-top-issues-facing-hr-excutives-our-predictions-for-2019?utm_source=Eloqua&utm_medium=email&utm_campaign=0001_UnlockingPowerPpl&utm_content=email1

Burke, W., & Litwin, G. (1992). A causal model of organizational performance and change. *Journal of Management, 18*(3), 523-545.

Byrne, Z. S. (2015). *Understanding employee engagement: Theory, research, and practice.* New York: Routledge.

Cameron, K. S., & Quinn, R. E. (1999). *Diagnosing and changing organizational culture.* New York: Addison-Wesley.

Cameron, K. S., & Quinn, R. E. (2011). *Diagnosing and changing organizational culture* (3rd edn.). San Francisco: Jossey-Bass.

Cappelli, P., & Eldor, L. (2019, May 17). Where measuring engagement goes wrong. *Harvard Business Review* blog. Retrieved from https://hbr.org/2019/05/where-measuring-engagement-goes-wrong

Chemers, M. M. (1997). *An integrative theory of leadership.* Mahwah, NJ: Lawrence Elrbaum Associates.

Chemers, M. M., Watson, C. B., & May, S. T. (2000). "Dispositional affect and leadership effectiveness: A comparison of self-esteem, optimism, and efficacy." *Personality and Social Psychology Bulletin, 26*(3), 267-277.

Chen, G., & Bliese, P. D. (2002). "The role of different levels of leadership in predicting self- and collective efficacy: Evidence for discontinuity." *Journal of Applied Psychology, 87*(3), 549-556.

Cherniss, C., & Adler, M. (2000). *Promoting emotional intelligence in organizations.* Alexandria, VA: ASTD.

Church, A. (2013). Engagement is in the eye of the beholder: Understanding differences in the OD vs. talent management mindset. *OD Practitioner, 45*(2), 42-48.

Claydon, R. (2019, January 20). Posts. [LinkedIn page]. Retrieved from https://www.linkedin.com/feed/update/urn:li:activity:6493032987150639104

Cohen, J. (1992). A power primer. *Psychological Bulletin, 112*, 155-159.

Cooper, R. K., & Sawaf, A. (1997). *Executive EQ: Emotional Intelligence in leadership and organizations.* New York: Peregee.

Coutu, D. L. (2002). "How resilience works." *Harvard Business Review, 80*(5), 46-50, 52, 55.

Csikszentmihalyi, M. *Flow: The psychology of optimal experience.* New York: Harper & Row.

Deci, E. L., & Ryan, R. M. (1985). *Intrinsic motivation and self-determination in human behavior.* New York: Plenum.

Deci, E. L., & Ryan, R. M. (2000). The "what" and "why" of goal pursuits: Human needs and the self-determination of behavior. *Psychological Inquiry: An international journal for the advancement of psychological theory, 11*(4), 227-268.

Deming, W. E. (1986) *Out of the crisis.* Cambridge, MA: Massachusetts Institute of Technology, Center for Advanced Engineering Study.

Denison, D. R. (1990). *Corporate culture and organizational effectiveness*. New York: Wiley.

Eby, L. T., Freeman, D. M., Rush, M. C., & Lance, C. E. (1999). Motivational bases of affective organizational commitment: A partial test of an integrative theoretical model. *Journal of Occupational and Organizational Psychology, 72*(4), 463-483.

Eden, D., & Aviram, A. (1993). Self-efficacy training to speed reemployment: Helping people to help themselves. *Journal of Applied Psychology, 78*(3), 352-360.

Eisenberger, R., Cummings, J., Armeli, S., & Lynch, P. (1997). Perceived organizational support, discretionary treatment, and job satisfaction. *Journal of Applied Psychology, 82*(5), 812-820.

Eisenberger, R., Fasolo, P., & and David-LaMastro, V. (1990). Perceived organizational support and employee diligence, commitment, and innovation. *Journal of Applied Psychology, 75*(1), 51-59.

Eisenberger, R., Huntingdon, R., Hutchinson, S., & Sowa, D. (1986). Perceived organizational support. *Journal of Applied Psychology, 71*(3), 500-508.

Ford, J. D., Ford, L. W., & D'Amelio, A. (2008). Resistance to change: The rest of the story. *Academy of Management Review, 33*(2), 362-377.

Fornal. P. (2002). *Developing and sustaining a high-performance organizational culture*. SHRM Information Center. [Cannot locate].

Foster, R. D. (2010). "Resistance, justice, and commitment to change." *Human Resource Development Quarterly, 21*(1), 3-39.

Frankl, V. E. (1959; 2006). *Man's search for meaning*. Boston: Beason Press.

Franz, A. (2019, February 1). "What Exactly Is the Employee Experience?" *Forbes* blog. Retrieved from https://www.forbes.com/sites/forbescoachescouncil/2019/02/01/what-exactly-is-the-employee-experience/#3baddf7c4dbf

Frayne, C., & Latham, G. (1987). "Application of social learning theory to employee self-management of attendance." *Journal of Applied Psychology, 72*(3), 387-392.

Gallup (2017). "State of the American Workplace."

Gagné, M., Koestner, R., & Zuckerman, M. (2000). "Facilitating acceptance of organizational change: The importance of self-determination." *Journal of Applied Sociology, 30*(9), 1843-1852.

Garland, H., & Adkinson, J. (1987). "Standards, persuasion, and performance: A test of cognitive mediation theory." *Group & Organizational Studies, 12*(2), 208-220.

Gelfand, M. J., Leslie, L. M., Keller, K., & de Dreu, C. (2012). "Conflict cultures in organizations: How leaders shape conflict cultures and their organizational-level consequences." *Journal of Applied Psychology, 97*(6), 1131-1147.

Giles, S. (2018, May 9). How VUCA is reshaping the business environment, and what it means for innovation. Forbes blog. Retrieved from https://www.forbes.com/sites/sunniegiles/2018/05/09/how-vuca-is-reshaping-the-business-environment-and-what-it-means-for-innovation/#ef20102eb8d5

Gist, M. (1987). Self-efficacy: Implications for organizational behavior and human resource management. *Academy of Management Review, 12*(3), 472-485.

Gist, M., & Mitchell, T. (1992). Self-efficacy: A theoretical analysis of its determinants and malleability. *Academy of Management Review*, 17(2), 183-211.

Goddard, R. D., Hoy, W. K., & Hoy, A. W. (2004). Collective efficacy beliefs: Theoretical developments, empirical evidence, and future directions. *Educational Researcher, 33*(3), 3-13.

Godkin, L. (2008). Institutional change, absorptive capacity, and the organizational zone of inertia. *Human Resource Development Review, 7*(2), 184-197.

Goleman, D. (1998). *Working with emotional intelligence.* New York: Bantam.

Griffin, M. A., Parker, S. K., & Mason, C. M. (2010). Leader vision and the development of adaptive and proactive performance: A longitudinal study. *Journal of Applied Psychology, 95*(1), 174-182.

Groyserg, B., & Slind, M. (2012). Leadership is a conversation. *Harvard Business Review, 90*(6), 76-84, 144.

Guthrie, J. P., & Schwoerer, C. E. (1994). Individual and contextual influences on self-assessed training needs. *Journal of Organizational Behavior, 15*(5), 405-422.

Harter, J. K., Schmidt, F. L., & Hayes, T. L. (2002). Business-unit-level relationship between employee satisfaction, employee engagement, and business outcomes: A meta-analysis. *Journal of Applied Psychology, 87*(2), 268-279.

HayGroup. (2013). *Preparing for take-off: Global research into employee retention*. White paper. Philadelphia: Author.

Howell, W. C., & Dipboye, R. L. (1982). *Essentials of industrial and organizational psychology*. Homewood, IL: Dorsey.

Hughes, R. L., Ginnett, R. C., & Curphy, G. J. (1999). *Leadership: Enhancing the lessons of experience*. New York: Irwin McGraw-Hill.

Jex, S. M., & Gudanowski, D. M. (1992). Efficacy beliefs and work stress: An exploratory study. *Journal of Organizational Behavior, 13*(5), 509-517.

John, O. P., & Srivastava, S. (1999). The Big-Five trait taxonomy: History, measurement, and theoretical perspectives. In L. A. Pervin & O. P. John (Eds.), Handbook of personality: Theory and research (Vol. 2, pp. 102–138). New York: Guilford Press.

Judge, T. A., Thoresen, C. J., Bono, J. E., & Patton, G. K. (2001). The job satisfaction–job performance relationship: A qualitative and quantitative review. *Psychological Bulletin, 127*(3), 376-407.

Kaiser, R. B., Hogan, R., & Craig, S. B. (2008). Leadership and the fate of organizations. *American Psychologist, 63*(2), 96-110.

Kaplan, R. S., & Norton, D. P. (1996a). *The balanced scorecard: Translating strategy into action*. Boston: Harvard Business School Press.

Kaplan, R. S., & Norton, D. P. (1996b). Using the balanced scorecard as a strategic management system. *Harvard Business Review, 74*(1), 75-85.

Katz, D., & Kahn, R. L. (1978). *The social psychology of organizations* (2nd ed.). New York: Wiley.

Koestner, R., Ryan, R. M., Bernieri, F., & Holt, K. (1984). Setting limits on children's behavior: The differential effects of controlling vs. informational styles on intrinsic motivation and creativity. *Journal of Personality, 52*(3), 233-248.

Kopelman, R. E., Brief, A. P., & Guzzo, R. A. (1990). The role of climate and culture in productivity. In B. Schneider (Ed.), *Organizational climate and culture* (pp. 282-318). San Francisco: Jossey-Bass.

Kotter, J. P. (1990). *A force for change: How leadership differs from management*. New York: Free Press.

Kotter, J. (2011, June 14). Think you're communicating enough? Think again. *Forbes* blog. Retrieved from https://www.forbes.com/sites/johnkotter/2011/06/14/think-youre-communicating-enough-think-again/#3debd5236275

Kotter, J. P, & Heskett, J. (1992). *Corporate culture and performance*. New York: Free Press.

Kramer, R. M. (1999). Trust and distrust in organizations: Emerging perspectives, enduring questions. *Annual Review of Psychology, 50*(1), 569-598.

Labovitz, G., & Rosansky, V. (1997). *The power of alignment: How great companies stay centered and accomplish extraordinary things*. New York: John Wiley & Sons.

Lafley, A. G., & Martin, R. L. (2013). *Playing to win: How strategy really works*. Boston: Harvard Business Review Press.

Lau, R. S. M., & May, B. (1998). A win-win paradigm for quality of work life and business performance. *Human Resource Development Quarterly, 9*(3), 211-226.

Larson, C. E., & LaFasto, F. M. J., (1989*) Teamwork: What must go right; what can go wrong.* Newbury Park, CA: Sage.

Lee, K., & Allen, N. J. (2002). Organizational citizenship behavior and workplace deviance: The role of affect and cognitions. *Journal of Applied Psychology, 87*(1), 131-142.

Lee, T. H., & Cosgrove, T. (2014, June). Engaging doctors in the health care revolution. *Harvard Business Review, 92*(6), 104-111, 138.

Lencioni, P. M. (2012). The advantage: Why organizational health trumps everything else in business. San Francisco: Josey-Bass.

Lent, R., Brown, S., & Larkin, K. (1987). Comparison of three theoretically derived variables in predicting career and academic behavior: Self-efficacy, interest congruence, and consequence thinking. *Journal of counseling psychology, 34*(3), 293-298.

Lucas, J. R. (1999). *The passionate organization: Igniting the fire of employee commitment.* New York: AMACOM.

MacMillan, J., Elliot, E. E., & Serfaty, D. (2009). Communication overhead: The hidden cost of team cognition. In E. Salas & S. M. Fiore (Eds.), *Team cognition: Understanding the factors that drive process and performance* (pp. 61-82). Washington D. C.: American Psychological Association Press.

Maddux, J. E. (1995). Self-efficacy theory. In J. E. Maddux (ed.), *Self-efficacy, adaptation, and adjustment.* The Plenum Series in Social/Clinical Psychology. Boston: Springer.

Martocchio, J. (1994). Effects of conceptions of ability on anxiety, self-efficacy, and learning in training. *Journal of Applied Psychology, 79*(6), 819-825.

McCroskey, J. C., & Richmond, V. P. (1985). *Communication: Apprehension, avoidance, and effectiveness.* Scottsdale, AZ: Gorsuch Scarisbrick.

McCroskey, J. C., & Richmond, V. P. (1990). Willingness to communicate: A cognitive view. *Journal of Social Behavior and Personality, 5*(2), 19-37.

McDonald, T., & Siegall, M. (1992). The effects of technological self-efficacy and job focus on job performance, attitudes, and withdrawal behaviors. *Journal of Psychology, 126*(5), 465-475.

Miller, D. (2001). Successful change leaders: What makes them? What do they do that is different? *Journal of Change Management, 2*(4), 359-368.

Miller, G. A. (2015). *Learning the language of addiction counseling* (4th ed.). Hoboken, NJ: John Wiley & Son.

Morrison, R., & Brantner, T. (1992). What enhances or inhibits learning a new job? A basic career issue. *Journal of Applied Psychology, 71*(6), 926-940.

Muchiri, M. (2010, December). Societal culture as a moderator of the impact of leadership on organizational effectiveness: A conceptual model. In B. Gurd (ed.), *Proceedings of Managing for Unknowable Futures: 24th Annual Australian and New Zealand Academy of Management Conference* (pp. 1-15), Adelaide, Australia.

Muchiri, M., & Ayoko, O. (2013). Linking demographic diversity to organisational outcomes. *Leadership & Organization Development Journal, 34*(5), 384-406.

Muchiri, M. & Cooksey, R. (2008, December). Leadership viewed through double lenses: an examination of transformational leader behaviours and social processes of leadership and their impact on key organisational variables within Australian local councils. In M. Wilson (ed.), *Proceedings of Australian and New Zealand Academy of Management 22nd ANZAM Conference: Managing in the Pacific Century* (pp. 1-22), Auckland, New Zealand.

Muchiri, M., & Cooksey, R. (2011). Examining the effects of substitutes for leadership on performance outcomes. *Leadership & Organization Development Journal, 32*(8), 817-836.

Muchiri, M., Cooksey, R., & Walumbwa, F. (2012). Transformational and social processes of leadership as predictors of organisational outcomes. *Leadership & Organization Development Journal, 33*(7), 662-683.

Myers, K. (2012, April). *Immunity to change management.* Presentation to the ACMP Global Conference, Las Vegas, GA.

Nadler, D. A. (1976). The use of feedback for organizational change: Promises and pitfalls. *Group & Organization Studies, 1*(2), 177-186.

Nadler, D. A., & Tushman, M. L. (1989). Organizational frame bending: Principles for managing reorientation. *Academy of Management Executive, 3*(3), 194-204.

Nadler, D. A., & Tushman, M. L. (1990). Beyond the charismatic leader: Leadership and organizational change. *California Management Review, 32*(2), 77-97.

Nesterkin, D. (2013). Organizational change and psychological reactance. *Journal of Organizational Change, 26*(3), 573-592.

Ng, K.-Y., Ang, S., & Chan, K.-Y. (2008). Personality and leader effectiveness: A moderated mediation model of leadership self-efficacy, job demands, and job autonomy. *Journal of Applied Psychology, 93*(4), 733-743.

OCAI Online. (n.d.). Organizational Culture Assessment Instrument. Retrieved from http://www.ocai-online.com/

Organ, D. W. (1990). The motivational basis of organizational citizenship behavior. In L. L. Cummings & B. M. Staw (Eds.), *Research in organizational behavior* (Vol. 12; pp. 43-72). Greenwich, CT: JAI Press.

Pierce, J. L., Gardner, D. G., Cummings, L. L., & Dunham, R. B. (1989). Organization-based self-esteem: Construct definition, measurement, and validation. *Academy of Management Journal, 32*(3), 622-648.

Posner, J. M., & Kouzes, B. Z. (1987). *The leadership challenge: How to get extraordinary things done in organizations.* San Francisco: Jossey-Bass.

Pritchard, R., Jones, D., Roth, P., Steubing, K., & Ekeberg, S. (1988). Effects of group feedback, goal setting, and incentives on organizational productivity. *Journal of Applied Psychology Monograph, 73*(2), 337-358.

Quinn, R. E., & Rohrbaugh, J. (1983). A spatial model of effectiveness criteria: Towards a competing values approach to organizational analysis. *Management Science, 29*(3), 273-393.

Reeves, M., Fæste, L., Whitaker, K., & Hassan, F. (2018, January 31). The truth about corporate transformation. *MIT Sloan Management Review* blog. Retrieved from https://sloanreview.mit.edu/article/the-truth-about-corporate-transformation/

Riggs, M., Warka, J., Babasa, B., Betancourt, R., & Hooker, S. (1994). Development and validation of self-efficacy and outcome expectancy scales for job-related applications. *Educational and Psychological Measurement, 54*(3), 793-802.

Rock, D., & Schwartz, J. (2006, June). The neuroscience of leadership. *strategy+business, 43.*

Rosenstein, L. S., Sadun, R., & Jena, A. B. (2018, October 17). Why doctors need leadership training. *Harvard Business Review.* Retrieved from https://hbr.org/2018/10/why-doctors-need-leadership-training

Rousseau, D. (1990). Assessing organizational culture: The case for multiple methods. In B. Schneider (Ed.), *Organizational climate and culture* (pp. 153-192). San Francisco: Jossey-Bass.

Rummler, G., & Brache, A. (1995). *Improving performance: How to manage the white space on the organization chart.* San Francisco: John Wiley & Sons.

Ryan, R. M., & Deci, E. L. (2000). Self-determination theory and the facilitation of intrinsic motivation, social development, and well-being. *American Psychologist, 55*(1), 68-78.

Ryan, K. D., & Oestreich, D. K. (1998). *Driving fear out of the workplace: Creating the high-trust, high-performance organization* (2nd ed.). San Francisco: Jossey-Bass.

Sadri, G., & Robertson, I. (1993). Self-efficacy and work-related behavior: A meta-analysis. *Applied Psychology: An International Review, 42*(2), 139-152.

Saks, A. M. (1994). Moderating effects of self-efficacy for the relationship between training method and anxiety and stress reactions of newcomers. *Journal of Organizational Behavior, 15*(7), 639-654.

Shamir, B (1990). Calculations, values and identities: the sources of collectivistic work motivation. *Human Relations,* 43(4), 313-332.

Schaufeli, W. B. (2012). Work engagement: What do we know and where do we go? *Romanian Journal of Applied Psychology, 14*(1), 3-10.

Schaufeli, W. B., Salanova, M., González-Romá, & Bakker, A. B. (2002). The measurement of engagement and burnout: A two sample confirmatory factor analytic approach. *Journal of Happiness Studies, 3*(1), 71-92.

Schneider, B., Hanges, P., Smith, D., & Salvaggio, A. (2003). Which comes first, employee attitudes or organizational and financial performance? *Journal of Applied Psychology, 88* (5), 836-851.

Senge, P. M. (1990). *The fifth discipline: The art and practice of the learning organization.* New York: Currency-Doubleday.

Shamir, B (1990). Calculations, values, and identities: The sources of collectivistic work motivation. *Human Relations, 43*(4), 313-332.

Shea, G. B., & Guzzo, R. A. (1987). Group effectiveness: What really matters? *Sloan Management Review, 28*(3), 25-31.

Steers, R. M. (1977). Antecedents and outcomes of organizational commitment. *Administrative Science Quarterly, 22*(1), 46-56.

Sternberg, R. J. (1997) Successful Intelligence: how practical and creative intelligence determine success in life. NY: Penguin/Putnam.

Stumpf, S. A., Brief, A. P., & Hartman, K. (1987). Self-efficacy expectations and coping with career-related events. *Journal of Vocational Behavior, 31*(1), 91-108.

Szabla, D. B. (2007). A multidimensional view of resistance to organizational change: Exploring cognitive, emotional, and intentional responses to planned change across perceived change leadership strategies. *Human Resource Development Quarterly, 18*(4), 525-558.

Thompson, K., & Luthans, F. (1990). Organizational culture: A behavioral perspective. In B. Schneider (Ed.), *Organizational climate and culture* (pp. 319-344). San Francisco: Jossey-Bass.

Truske, S. D. (1999). *Leadership in high performance organizational cultures.* Westport, CT: Quorum.

Ulrich, D. (1998). A new mandate for Human Resources. *Harvard Business Review, 76*(1), 124-134.

Vince, R. (2002). The impact of emotion on organizational learning. *Human Resource Development International, 5*(1), 73-85.

Wakeman, C. (2017). *No ego: How leaders can cut the cost of workplace drama, end entitlement, and drive big results.* New York: St. Martin's Press.

Waldersee, R. (1994). Self-efficacy and performance as a function of feedback sign and anxiety: A service experiment. *Journal of Applied Behavioral Science, 30*(3), 346-356.

Weingart, L., & Weldon, E. (1991). Processes that mediate the relationship between a group goal and group member performance. *Human Performance, 4*(1), 33-54.

Wissema, J. (2000). Offensive change management with the step-by-step method. *Journal of Change Management, 1*(4), 332-343.

Wood, R., and Bandura, A. (1989). Impact of conceptions of ability on self-regulatory mechanisms and complex decision-making skills. *Journal of Personality and Social Psychology, 56*(3), 407-415.

Zaccaro, S. J., Gualtieri, J., (1995) "Task cohesion as a facilitator of team decision making under temporal urgency." *Military Psychology, 7(2),* 77-93.

Made in the USA
Las Vegas, NV
12 March 2022

45519625R00125